Why Life Events Are Predestined
and How Our Universe Originated

Why Life Events Are Predestined

And How Our Universe Originated

Pia Pikwah Fields

In memory of my dear mother, Lam Hapwah,
my father Chan, Pao Kwong, and my
great grandmother Li.

Their souls in heaven will give me strength to achieve my goal.

Contents

Part Two: Data

Part Three: After This Book Was Published Online

Foreword

A good book makes you think and a great book makes you think and rethink both old beliefs and new concepts, leaving you wiser in the process. By this definition, *Why Life Events Are Predestined and How Our Universe Originated* is a great book. Pikwah Fields presents a scientific argument to explain astrology, paranormal events, precognition, and even the resurrection of Jesus Christ.

Whether you agree with Pikwah's theories or are unwilling to accept her arguments that are based on physics for predestination, you will be forced by the thoroughness of her research and the reasonableness of her arguments to at least consider what this first-time author has to say about the origin of the universe and events that have occurred since. This is not light reading, but it is enlightening. Open the pages as you would a scholarly tome, study the text carefully, and prepare yourself to become engrossed in an intriguing, passionate, and verifiable explanation about why most of life's mysteries—both on a cosmic and individual level—have already been answered.

—*Ellen Singer,* Author of New York Times bestseller
Don't Eat the Marshmallow—Yet

About this Book

From 1978 to 1984, I worked with a fortune teller, Tong Kang Jie, in Hong Kong and watched him pull predictions from a book, *Tie Ban Shen Suan* (铁板神算). That book was written by an ancient Chinese astronomer, Shao Kang Jie (邵康节), one thousand years ago. Mr. Shao did what Isaac Newton could not do—used formulas to predict events that happened in our lives. Based on an individual's birth time, he could figure out the birth years of that person's family members, their personalities, and even their life experiences. All the outcomes were recorded in his book without exception. It was as if they were carved on an iron plate (铁板) and could not be changed.

As a witness, I couldn't help but contemplate why life events are predestined and what causes people's good luck or bad luck. I believe it must have something to do with quantum mechanics—particles floating invisibly in the air. I recorded all of Shao's amazing predictions in this book, along with some discussions about physics and paranormal events.

The Chinese believe that our universe is composed of five elements, which are categorized by either yin or yang (阴阳五). Yang represents physical things that can be detected and have been recognized by traditional scientists. Yin represents subatomic energy, which carries the five elements and changes according to the rotation of the planets. I would like to call that "time traits." The trait at our birth time constructs our life frame (aura). Aura is as unique as our fingerprints or DNA. It is impacted by the changing universal time traits and influences the function of our physical bodies. A harmonious interaction creates good luck, and a conflicting interaction causes bad luck. A strong and balanced aura can bring us a successful life. Since planetary movements are predestined, life events—created by the interaction of time traits—are also predestined.

With the concept of invisible Yin, we can explain many so-called paranormal events. That is why I discussed them in my book as well.

I also believe that the Chinese Yin-Yang (five-element) theory is the ultimate law that can explain all the phenomena in different scales of our universe. Our physicists first adopted Newton's laws, then recognized Einstein's theory, and finally hoped quantum mechanics would be the ultimate theory. Up to today, none of the above theories can provide a complete explanation. Meanwhile, scientists tend to ignore the many paranormal events that happen in our daily lives.

Our scientists only recognize things that can be detected by particle detectors. They thus ignore Yin, an invisible existence. I believe, just as biologists admit that borrowing energy can create basic elements in biology, our universe was created from nothing—a transformation from Yin to Yang. I sent my book to Stephen Hawking when I first published it in 2001. I remember that after I kept sending him emails, his secretary told me the book would be read within a few days. In 2010, he published *The Grand Design* and announced that "the universe can and will create itself from nothing." His statement aligns with the Chinese Yin-Yang theory I introduced in my book: this universe could originate from nothing—not just the Big Bang.

We are compromised in some way. However, as Stephen Hawking simply told scientists not to invoke God, I try to make scientists recognize that God, spirits, and ETs are scientific existences on the Yin scale. The physical world they recognize is just part of the universe. Please excuse my discussion on the origin of our universe. My original goal was to research how and why life events are predestined. When I noticed that the Big Bang theory was being promoted by our physicists in a seemingly ridiculous way, I introduced them to Chinese Yin-Yang theories and used those to explain the universe's origin.

With the concept of Yin, I challenged Einstein's theory in this way: when particles travel faster than light (such as in tunneling or Hawking radiation), they could reject the graviton. Without gravity acting on them, the particle's mass turns to zero, making Einstein's formula $E=mc^2$ lose its meaning. The infinite situation Einstein assumed never existed, and we didn't need to create a Big Bang story to complete his theory. Some scientists have expressed doubt about such an infinity concept as well.

In my book, I used Stephen Hawking's baby universe theory and Hawking radiation to interpret spirits and supernormal events. Such interpretations make Mr. Hawking's theories more practical and greater. I believe that God showed miracles through Stephen Hawking by giving him a longer life—just as God let Jesus be resurrected. It is unbelievable for science, but it is a simple truth in the Chinese Yin-Yang theory.

Physicists also wonder how to unify the four forces in physics. I point out that without the graviton involved, the electromagnetic force, strong force, and weak force will not function within mass. Under such conditions, mass can exist as "nothing" and may be able to travel faster than light.

The most important contribution of this book is combining science and religion. When all the gods actually exist scientifically, we have no reason to fight over who is fake and who is real. The only thing we need to do is behave ourselves, because all gods are more powerful than humanity. Without a science degree, I jumped in to discuss these matters because the topic is so important. It relates to the peace of our world, which is filled with religious conflict and fighting.

I am also concerned with how to use scientific and philosophical concepts to influence our lives—not just discuss them in an academic context. I care more about how to manage our world than how it was originated. That's why, when I republished this book in 2010, I couldn't help but discuss the things that were happening in the world at the time. I promoted a new concept for evaluating a successful life: people who can use the minimum material resources to maintain maximum joy are successful—not those who earn high salaries like robots and spend money like fools.

I covered many topics in this book and have many hopes for it. However, since I lacked knowledge and funding to promote it, the book did not sell well. Things did not happen as the psychics predicted. I did what I promised: closed the book and went home in 2012. I didn't even know the book was no longer available because its printing house had shut down.

In 2019, I published my second book, *An Appeal to the US Supreme Court and a Proposal to Our President*. I simply turned a brief and appendix into a book that was related to a court case involving a ten-million-dollar testament. The psychic Jenny's predictions came true. That made me think about republishing and promoting this book again.

My second book disclosed how a group of criminals used a forged will to steal nine million dollars from a 96-year-old blind man and his family, which included three individuals with mental illnesses. Courts in the United States allowed them to do it.

Since I have to spend several thousand dollars on the campaign to promote the court case, I decided to republish this book as well, using one fund to promote both books.

This book, *Why Life Events Are Predestined and How Our Universe Originated*, covers many topics. It not only discusses how the universe originated but also addresses how to manage the world.

How to help 8 billion people survive in a decent way is the top priority. We need to adopt both socialist concepts (distribution and discipline) and capitalist concepts (freedom and profit) to manage our world. We must eliminate the conflict between the two systems and save money from wars. We should abandon the capitalist focus on consumption and competition, as it only creates debt and conflict. We have to minimize costs and reduce working hours to enjoy life and friendships.

From Yin-Yang theory, I developed a philosophy: the sum of a person's fortune, happiness, and health is fixed, based on the structure of their aura. One cannot receive more than their aura can sustain. Excessive fortune may come at the cost of love or health.

Most of the world's problems are caused by human greed: war, financial crises, healthcare deficits, wealth inequality, the refugee crisis, and government debt. I hope the theories above can help people take a new approach to life.

We don't rely on taxing the rich to help the poor, as Western governments do. We also don't encourage the poor to take power and strip wealth from the rich, as communist governments have done. We simply tell people to behave, because entities beyond this world truly exist and are watching everything we do. I advise people to make wise choices. Again, since our aura cannot sustain more than we deserve, it makes no sense to sacrifice love, happiness, and health for excessive fortune.

I would like to express my appreciation to my sister, Eva Yi-Wah Chan, who generously gave this book a final and careful edit for free. I also appreciate her former husband, Dr. Cheung, a lifetime physics professor at CUNY. He referred me to the Yin-Yang symbol that Niels Bohr used in his coat of arms. Bohr and his student were inspired by Shao Kang Jie's book, *Wang Ji Jing Shi Tu.* I am grateful to Ellen Singer, author of the New York Times bestseller *Don't Eat the Marshmallow—Yet!*, who gave me a powerful book review—though unfortunately, few people understood her meaning. Finally, I am grateful to my ex-husband, Richard Fields, who gave me the first edit when the book was originally written in broken English.

In my two books—one fighting for justice and revealing the truth about our courtrooms, and the other declaring a truth that life is predestined—I touched on the two things philosopher Bertrand Russell sought his entire life. I followed his principles in guiding my own life. I want to announce once more: our life events are predestined, based on our birth time traits. They were recorded in a book (*Tie Ban Shen Suan*) by the Chinese astronomer Shao Kang Jie one thousand years ago. The sum of what we can gain in life is fixed. We cannot sustain more than we deserve. We should make smart decisions before it's too late.

June 1st, 2025, in New York

Part One

Theory

Amazing Predictions from Ancient China

Are there any correlations between the rotations of the planets and human behavior? Are events in our lives predestined to happen? Is it possible to predict the occurrence of future events? After Tycho Brahe (1546–1601), Johannes Kepler (1571–1630), and Isaac Newton (1642–1727), scientists no longer discussed these subjects. For them, things they could not explain are nonscientific and superstitious.

Johannes Kepler was the first astronomer to determine and prove that planets move in ellipses. He also believed that certain casual connections do exist between planetary movements and human behaviors. Some accurate predictions Kepler made prove his opinion. Still he was unable to connect them with a formula.

It is said that many discussions in Isaac Newton's manuscripts were related to esoteric theology. Unfortunately, Newton never attained any conclusion between the rotation of the planets and the events on earth.

In the eleventh century (1011–1077), Chinese astronomer Shao Kang Jie (邵康节) also researched astrology. The calendar system he set up included 129,600 years. His calendar and formula were able to predict an individual's life. Basing on that individual's birth minutes, it has a group of numbers to help us pick sentences in Shao's book, *Tie Ban Shen Suan*. Those sentences revealed our education, career, and marital backgrounds.

They described our parents' personalities and occupations. They even listed the birth years of our direct family members. In this book, I will briefly introduce Shao Kang Jie's amazing accomplishments and then discuss why life events are predetermined.

In 1978, coincidently, I got a reading from Mr. Tong, a person who knew Shao Kang Jie's formula. I invited my friend Lung to get the reading as well for testing the accuracy of Shao Kang Jie's predictions. According to Shao's theory, people who were born five minutes apart will have different lives. Lung only knew that he was born around five in the morning, and Mr. Tong had to verify his birth minute first. The first three sentences Mr. Tong pulled out did not match Lung's case. The fourth sentence sounded right, and it said that people who were born at this moment must have his father dead and have his mother alive. However, Mr. Tong said if his father died within three years, it still will not count. Since Lung's father passed way for only two years, Mr. Tong had to continue his calculation. Sentence related to the next fifteen minutes said that a person who was born at that moment must be a twin. I never knew that Lung was a younger twin.

Based on that fifteen-minute interval, Mr. Tong composed a series of numbers and told us according to those numbers to pick up sentences from *Tie Ban Shen Suan*. All the predictions must match Lung's case without variation. For example, the next sentence said that Lung's father kept his eyes open after died. During the Cultural Revolution, the twins were exiled to a farm in Hainan Island. They were not allowed to say farewell to their dying father. For that reason, his father refused to close his eyes when died. We were surprised that such an unusual scenario on a deathbed was mentioned in a book nine hundred years ago and showed that it was destiny.

Up to today I still wonder—the previous prediction belonged to Long's older brother. His father died less than three years if he was with us that day and requested a reading. How would Mr. Tong handle the case? Did Shao Kang Jie even know who would read his book at when?

At my request, I got a chance to learn and work with Mr. Tong. For eight years he taught me all the knowledge of astrology that he knew, except Shao Kang Jie's formula. He worried that if I knew it, I would disclose that to the whole world and violate the rule his teacher set up. He did not pass his knowledge to anybody until he died. The last time I saw Tong work was 1997 in my apartment in New York. One of our clients told us that he was a waiter, but the book said his specialty was economics. The client then admitted that his major in college was economics.

Another client told us that he was a stockbroker. However, the book said that his specialty was business management. The client then told us that he had a bachelor degree in business management.

My friend Lang was a life insurance agent then. The book said he belonged to the field of garments. It was true that time he also owned garment factory. The book also said that Lang would work with blueprints. Lang did have a bachelor degree in engineering. However, Lang had only two years of engineering experience in America. As a Chinese immigrant at his forties and with farsightedness, Lang never imagined he could have an engineering job. Amazingly, a few years later, Lang passed a technician exam and now has a good-paying job in the New York City Subway system (MTA). He will deal with blueprints for the rest of his life like what Shao predicted in *Tie Ban Shen Suan*.

The book also said that one of our clients was supposed to work for the government. It was interesting that the man first served in the US military and then worked for the US Postal Service. He did not work in private companies for even one day.

Another client claimed that his father was an art professor, but the book said his father got paid by the government. He then realized that the college his father worked for belonged to the Taiwan government. We once pulled out a sentence indicating the death year of a client's mother.

One of my readers told me that from *Tie Ban Shen Suan* he knew that his mother was not his biological mother. The book also amazingly indicated what year his father-in-law had a son born, what year the son died, and what year his second son was born (but was not as intelligent as the first one). This person got a reading from another master, but not from my teacher, Mr. Tong. He contacted me when he read my articles introducing *Tie Ban Shen Suan*. He told me that he had Shao's prediction for each season in his whole life. In 1996 the prediction warned him that he should act carefully before doing anything. Still he could not help fighting with his boss, and he lost his job. The book predicted that he would have a windfall in the following season. He did get a few thousand dollars in compensation from a lawsuit related to the apartment he rented. When he talked to me on the phone, he was still unemployed, which agreed with another prediction. It said that his experience was just like a flower in a storm. He couldn't wait to talk to me because the predictions were so amazing that nobody believed what he said.

My friend told me his friend got a sentence from *Tie Ban Shen Suan* saying that she was still a virgin after getting married. She did not have sex with her husband on their wedding night. Nobody knew that, but it was printed in the book that was written nine hundred years ago.

In 2018, I asked my friend to request a *Tie Ban Shen Suan* reading from another master in Hong Kong, Jiang Tian Yi (江天逸). He checked my birth minute, as what is needed to be done first. A sentence said that if I was born at that moment, I had a husband twelve years younger than me. The mention perfectly matched my situation. After that the master pulled out eleven sentences from Shao's book related to the birth years of my family members, five siblings, two parents, one son, and two husbands. He did it within ten minutes by phone call between New York and Hong Kong.

Stephen Hawking felt sorry and commented that today, most of our scientists are busy describing what the universe is, then ask the question why? Shao Kang Jie is the person who knew why. Otherwise he could not accurately predict human behaviors by using figures, formulas, and I-Jing hexagrams. Shao Kang Jie was very famous at his age. A few times the emperor offered him good positions in the palace.

He rejected it and worked as a teacher all his life. He opened schools to promote his formulas for people from all over the country. It looked like he knew that this world would lose track of his theory, and his worry was proven correct. Today, most Chinese have never heard of Shao. Only a few people in China know how to use Shao's formula, and none of them know how his system works. Scientists from high class rejected any fact that the scientific world could not explain. For them, more people from the low class believing in that means that it is superstitious.

Shao Kang Jie's system and formula were able to be mastered by his students for centuries. That means it was knowledge but not psychic ability. Human beings never have such a complete system to predict an individual's future and his behavior. It is said the original *Tie Ban Shen Suan* contained 170,000 different predictions. Unfortunately, the editions we can find in the books today usually have about twelve thousand predictions. Only a few people in China know the formula, and predictions they used were about only six thousand.

Fortunately, and unfortunately, within eight years, I saw how amazing Shao's predictions worked. As a witness, I just cannot shrug my responsibility to publicize the truth that I know. I have spent thirty years to contemplate why life events are predestined, spent ten years to learn English, and spent ten years to write and promote this book. I ran around to announce a truth that people hardly know and acted like an idiot. For comforting myself I consider things this way: One thousand years have already passed and people do not know Shao's achievement. Why should we mind to wait for another few hundred years or more? After the year 2010, I covered this book, went home, and put it away for almost ten years. Now I promote it together with a court case. If we are rejected by the US Supreme Court, I might shut up again. If our world prefers to ignore Shao's system, then it must be destiny. Isn't it?

Psychics' Predicting

How come events in our lives happen just as what a book predicted nine hundred years ago? Are they predestined? What determines them? I have been considering this topic for years.

This is an age of science. At the beginning of the nineteenth century, there was a theory of scientific determinism suggesting that the evolution of the universe could be determined precisely by a set of scientific laws. Those laws only recognize events that are repeatable and that have only one precise outcome. Later, the uncertainty principle stated that an event is supposed to have a few outcomes, and things on a microscopic level can be predicted up to only a certain limit. Unfortunately, scientists still cannot tolerate the verity in astrologic predictions. Before passing away, Stephen Hawking announced that things in our universe can have different ways to development themselves, not as our scientists believe that 1+1 must be 2.

People tend to believe in the existence of a mountain without seeing it but would not believe a prediction regarding an avalanche on that mountain. A mountain is always somewhere, and its existence can be proven easily; however, the scenario of an avalanche cannot be constantly envisioned. Since an avalanche happens instantaneously, at a particular moment, people tend to consider that the occurrence is coincidental. They don't believe it until they see it. If they could travel through a time dimension and preencounter or reencounter the avalanche, they might accept that the avalanche, like the mountain, always existed in some time dimension of our universe. Unfortunately, people cannot travel through a time dimension. People's sense about future events usually are obtained from instincts, feelings, trances, dreams, tarot cards, when their subconscious is active, their conscious is down, etc. However, they are not sure if their feelings are correct, and they cannot control or reproduce their precognition. They cannot prove that they did have those precognitions as well. All are based on someone's own testimony, which are not accepted by our traditional scientists.

Let us take a look at an interesting prediction that was witnessed by thousands of readers. Fourteen years before the Titanic sank, a book, *The Voyage of the Titan*,[26] was published. Its author, Morgan Robertson, described a collision between a ship and icebergs in the Atlantic. The ship named *Titan* was eight hundred feet long, eighty-two and a half feet shorter than the real *Titanic*. Both the *Titanic* and the *Titan* could hold three thousand passengers. Both disasters happened in April. Both ships were considered unsinkable, and both were short of lifeboats. Besides the author of the book, a few people claimed that they had previewed the disaster. One passenger postponed his trip because he had previously dreamed about the sinking of the Titanic. When the Titanic was departing, a woman grabbed people next to her and cried, "Why don't you stop that ship? Don't you see it is going to sink?" Unfortunately, all the dreams or precognitions were considered someone's own testimony and were ignored, including the meaning of the amazing prediction in *The Voyage of the Titan*.

Precognition does not determine but just preview future events that already exist in some dimension of time. If we could, based on the principles of physics, explain what creates the scenario of events just like we explain what forms a mountain, then predicting the future would not sound that ridiculous. First, we have to discuss the concepts of past, present, and future.

Albert Einstein (1879–1955) believed that the interval of time is relative. If we view things from an inertial time frame that is in relativistic speed, the future can become the present. The lifespan of a creature is determined by how fast it is moving

Assume that an inertial time frame A has a relativistic speed, and people over there see that John committed suicide in Nancy's wedding party. People in inertial time frame B would only see Nancy get married but would not see John die until sometime later. Messages can be obtained ahead if people in inertial time frame A are able to tell people in inertial time frame B about John's death before the suicide scenario actually shows in the time frame B.

Such an assumption was supported by astronomical pheno-mena: when two planets collide far enough away from the earth and explode, we will see one explosion first and see the other explosion later. Things occur in this way because time distorts when a relativistic speed occurs. We call this time dilation. This is also because the speed of light is finite and a certain amount of time is necessary for light to reach us and for us to see the event. I would like to say that Albert Einstein's theory makes predicting the future sound reasonable. He once commented: "*The distinction between past, present, and future is only an illusion, however persistent.*"

Channels to the Past and Future

In our universe, are there time frames where entities watch what happen on earth? Are they able to see through our future events because the time frame we are in are from different scale? Do they have any way to contact us and tell us what will happen?

Albert Einstein's theory has been confirmed by astrophysics. Unfortunately, in the world of science, we are not able to create that inertial time frame, such as a spaceship with the speed of light, and from that spaceship we view events on earth. However, I believe such inertial time frames do exist not far from us and that world belongs to a ghost or spirit. If we are able to get there, we can envision scenarios in the past or future. Things happened all at one time over there. When we only see Nancy smiling, spirits can also see that John committed suicide in Nancy's party later because they can travel faster than light. When we are able to get in touch with spirits or our spirit travels in the dream ourselves, we can receive certain messages ahead.

Scientists refuse to believe in the existence of spirits because their particle detectors can hardly detect spirits. In my opinion, spirits have the same wavelengths as virtual particles. For that reason they cannot be pulled by gravity and don't carry mass or weight that caused by gravity. That is why they cannot be detected by the particle detector.

There are thousands of reports of recorded near-death experiences (NDEs). Those reports are amazingly similar and occur among many related people, who could actually prove the existence of spirits. Below I am going to list the common traits spirits have and discuss them.

NDEers usually feel themselves separated from their physical bodies and floating in the air. (Since spirits cannot be attracted by gravity, they can float in the air.) NDEers are able to go anywhere in the world instantly by just making a wish. The physical limitation of speed has no meaning in their world. (Not being pulled by gravity, spirits are able to travel long distances in a fraction of a second.) NDEers can easily penetrate solid objects, such as walls or the bodies of human beings without being noticed (spirits are subatomic particles that cannot be barricaded by a solid object).

1. Reviewing the past scenario in their life[12] was what the NDEer experienced. They said those reviews are shown all at once in great detail. They are full color, three dimensional, panoramic reviews without their present physical surroundings. NDEers felt that they actually went back to the past but could not change what had happened. They could actually tell how the others felt at the moment. Time is greatly compressed, and the measurement of time is different from the time that our watches keep. It only took seconds for NDEers to actually reexperience their whole lives. That is why NDEers could reexperience their entire life during the short moment when they were dead. (Spirits are able to travel faster than light, thus they can reach the scenario related to the past or future in the time dimension.)

2. Many NDEers went through very dark tunnels, and at the end of the tunnels was a totally different world. Over there, light was much brighter than anything NDEers had ever seen on earth. It was warm and vibrant, yet it did not hurt their eyes.

Actually, we can make a connection between near-death experiences and Stephen Hawking's theory. Let me compare them with the concepts of Hawking's radiation, baby universes, and imaginary time.

NDEers felt that it was difficult to join or contact the physical world when they were dead and existed as spirits. They could not get humans' attention even though they actually contact human's physical bodies.

Stephen Hawking believes that "if an astronaut fell into a black hole,[2] the particles that made up the astronaut's body would be 'recycled' or would reemerge in a baby universe—another region of the universe that cannot join our universe."

It is said that spirits strongly resemble their physical bodies and they can be easily recognized by their familiars. Stephen Hawking also claims that an astronaut would be emitted in the form of radiation *at about the same mass.*

Hawking's radiation theory states that the black hole is not black but has radiation. It suggests that if an astronaut fell into a black hole, his particles could escape from the event horizon (a boundary in space time) of the black hole and would be emitted into a baby universe. Later *the particles that composed him would join our physical world in another way.* This concept is similar to the concept of reincarnation.

Stephen Hawking's "imaginary time" also implied that we do not have to meet a singularity. Instead of facing a singularity in a black hole, the astronaut would have a new beginning after being emitted. In my opinion, reincarnation also means that death is not a singularity for us. Our spirits are able to exist after our physical death. They would return to new lives one day.

Stephen Hawking believes traveling in a black hole might cause a person to go back into the past. He regrets that astronauts would not be able to tell us their experiences in black holes because they would be physically crushed out of existence. I would like to suggest another possibility. What if things that pass through a black hole are not physical bodies but fragments of air (chi)? Since spirits exist as chi, we can assume that the spirit can avoid being crushed. When it returns to its physical body and they still remember their experience, things happen in the other world. That is similar to the baby universe Stephen Hawking described, that when physical bodies survive death, it is not easy for people to remember their experience being dead. Therefore, near-death experiences, such as passing through black tunnels, are very valuable. Unfortunately, physicists would rather end their research than continue to investigate all those claims. In their minds anything that cannot be explained by existing scientific tenets is supernatural.

It is said that when Hawking's radiation occurs, particles of positive energy do not necessarily follow particles of negative energy, and instead of annihilation, those particles separate. Some of them escape from the black hole at a speed faster than light, creating emissions. Stephen Hawking also believes that the gravitational field at the event horizon of a black hole is strong enough to turn things into virtual particles or change virtual particles into particles. This assumption agrees with the Chinese yin-yang theory. Taoist philosophers state that yin and yang undergoes metamorphoses into each other. Chinese people believe that spirits are yin. The physical body is yang.

Actually, when some chi gong practitioners practiced meditation, they had the experience of passing through black tunnels. My chi gong teacher, Wu Yi, does not believe in the existence of spirits. He told me that he could pass through a very dark place and reach outer space when he was practicing meditation.

Chi gong meditation can also bring practitioners back to the past. A Chinese chi gong master envisioned an ancient honorific arch in a schoolyard during meditation practice. He did research later and found that the place where he practices meditation did have an honorific arch a thousand years ago.

Both near-death experiences and meditation experiences have their scientific points. Hawking believes that certain particles can change to virtual particles inside a black hole that has strong gravity. If we consider that spirits detaching from their dead or living bodies switch between particles and virtual particles, then we can explain why NDEers experience passing through very dark or light tunnels.

Theoretical physicists must be upset to see Stephen Hawking's baby universe theory being applied to illustrate near-death and meditation experiences. All these years, they would rather end their research than answer questions that relate to supernatural events. My point is that if a theory ignores everyday events and only discusses things that never exist, such as the Big Bang, we cannot say that the theory is great no matter how beautiful it is.

It is time to recognize the world beyond the atom—a world made of chi and virtual particles. That world contains past and future events, ancestors' spirits, our subtle bodies, and God. The Chinese call that the world of yin. Over there the dimension of time and the function of gravity are different from what we have in this physics world. Entities and phenomena in the world of yin may seem supernatural to us. Communicating with spirits or getting into psychic voyages can help psychics foretell the future. Therefore, when I discuss the topic of prediction, I discuss spirits and chi.

Other Ways of
Predicting the Future

Souls not only detach from dead bodies, they also are able to detach from living bodies and take psychic voyages.

Since souls belong to another time frame, communicating with them can help us obtain future messages. In order to have psychic voyages, we have to shut down our consciousness, such as dreams, hypnotism, physical debilitation, or in meditation. That is why chi gong practitioners believe that practicing meditation can enforce psychic abilities.

In December 23, 1997, my apartment building, from the second floor to the sixth floor, was seriously damaged by fire. A tenant in the sixth floor told me that she had dreamed that fire twice previously. She even mentioned those dreams to her mother. After the accident, two of her coworkers reminded her that someone in their office also had a prediction about that fire. Their predictions could not be merely illusions since different people had it. That fire did exist in some time dimension and was caught by their subconscious in dreams. However, only on the night of December 23, 1997, visual photons on earth conveyed us visions of that fire.

In dreams, people might be able to communicate with departed people and obtain messages related to the future. Before my friend's mother met his father, she dreamed of her dead stepfather. He told her that a man named Mak Fei would become her husband. On the same night, one of her relatives also had the same dream and heard the same name said to her. A few days later, a man named Mak Fei came to the village and married my friend's mother. At that time, Mak Fei traveled around China to fight against the Japanese invaders. He never knew he would get into that small village and meet his wife there.

Someone can obtain future messages in trances. Morgan Robertson, author of *The Voyage of the Titan*, was a sailor when he wrote the book. Before he wrote it, he sat at the desk facing the ocean and waited to go into a kind of trance. In the trance, his hand automatically wrote down something, and that was the story of the *Titan*. I believe his book was a work done by a spirit. A spirit can travel in the dimension of time and foresee the tragedy of the *Titanic*. They used his hand to record what they see.

The great writer Mark Twain also told us his experience shows that he can travel in the time dimension. Once, he dreamed his twin brother lay in a nice coffin that they could not offer, and a red rose was placed on his chest. Not long after that his twin brother died on a trip. Some women admired his brother's handsome looks and donated a nice coffin to him. Things were the same as what he saw in the dream except the flower. It is amazing that a little bit later a woman appeared and put a red rose on the chest of his brother. It seemed that it was not he who created the scenario in his dream but he got into a scenario that was already somewhere.

If Mark Twain did travel in another dimension of time, he should be able to communicate with spirits as well. From there he got all the inspiration to finish the tremendous novels he published.

Besides dreams, trances, and meditation, people who are in a certain mental state can also encounter the past or future events. I read a medical record saying that a mental patient kept seeing certain trivial and insignificant past visions. Those visions might appear in reverse order, results shown before the causative factors. Those scenarios flash very quickly, one appearing on top of another. A long time has already passed when they review those visions, and their watching shows that the process lasted for only a few seconds. It is interesting that patients lost consciousness at that moment and can barely recall those flashed scenarios. Psychiatric theory believes that is a symptom of mental illness. In my opinion those people neither had illusions, nor were they crazy. It is their nervous special structure made them travel to the past or future where the scenario of events continues to exist.

All the processes that cause psychic's predictions, dreaming, hypnosis, trances and meditation are related to subconscious activities and involve a spirit world. Unfortunately, most scientists still do not accept the existence of spirits. This subject will be discussed again in the second part of the book. Right now I am going to discuss a scientific topic. In our universe, are there any particles able to travel faster than the speed of light? Can these particles make traveling in the time dimension become possible?

Physiology and Precognition

In our world, are there particles able to travel faster than the speed of light? When most scientists avoid discussing such a possibility, I state my opinion as below:

Physiological particles, driven by bioelectricity, could travel faster than light. This is why supernatural events, psychic voyages, clairvoyance, telekinesis, automatic writing, recognition, and telepathy are only involved with a psychic's biological power but not any physics power. When traveling in the time dimension, we can only view but not actually change the historical or future events we encounter.

We have to admit that the biotic world is much more complex than the physics world. Scientists can create any physical thing but not even one biological cell. They know the physics structures of almost everything but lack knowledge about the human brain. Our brain consists of one hundred million billion billion particles (one followed by twenty-seven zeros or one octillion) and more than one hundred kinds of neurotransmitters. Some of them are able to perform tasks in four dimensions.

Neurotransmitters are driven by bioelectricity. Let us see how fast they can run:

When we are triggered by a stimulus, it generates a nerve impulse, a zone of electrical charge that causes the cell membrane to release neurotransmitters. Vesicles that contain neurotransmitters cross synapses (the gap between nerve cells) and bind to specific receptor molecules. The binding then activates an electrical response in the next cell and makes the cell release its neurotransmitters. Neurotransmitters only fire one after another when they transfer messages.

Please picture how quickly a single neurotransmitter has to react. When our fingers get burned, we move it away instantly under the command of our brain. That means it only takes a microsecond for millions of neurons to convey the messages between our finger and our brain. The amazing point is they have to fire and finish their duty one after another. To calculate the individual neurotransmitter's speed, we have to use a microsecond divided by the number of neurotransmitters involved in the message conveying. Remember the reactions that relate to our subconscious are a few times faster than the response from a regular neuron system. That is why we have reason to assume that speed reflected in biology could be faster than the speed of light. That is why almost all the psychic ability are related to biology power.

A famous Western psychology professor, Joseph Rhines, spent a half century making more than a hundred thousand tests on card guessing. He wanted to prove that our neuron system could receive messages from a distance without any physical connection. He hoped that parapsychology could be considered a legitimate science. He said, "It would be unpardonable for the scientific world to overlook evidence of the supernormal in the world if there are such." However, no matter how hard Professor Rhines worked, members of the scientific world refused to give him recognition and accused him of cheating.

In 1979, Physicist John Archibald Wheeler (1911–2008), the physicist who originated the term *black hole*, launched a battle to move the study of parapsychology out of the scientific workshop. Wheeler declared openly, "If confident men can be sent to jail, we should feel under no obligation to lend the 'air of legitimacy' to parapsychology." Joseph Rhines died three months after the battle started. Our scientists could not send Rhines, a parapsychologist, to the jail—they sent him to hell. What they did was not better than what churches did in the Middle Ages—put the astronomers in fires.

The same phenomena were researched in the 1980s–1990s in China. A child, Tang Yu, could recognize Chinese characters by just placing them under her armpit. Chinese chi researchers later found that other children also had this psychic ability. Such ability can be obtained from practicing chi gong. Since then, a few top Chinese scientists, including the Father of the Chinese Hydrogen Bomb, Qian Xue Sheng, founded a new science and named it *human body sciences*.

The objectives of this leader group were to research chi gong ability, psychic ability, and healing ability. They reevaluated the potential power that is issued by chi gong internal exercise. They believe that energy reemitted from the human body relates to the subatomic scale and could lead our traditional science to a higher level. Such research was stopped at the end of the 1990s.

To sum up my theory, the scenarios related to the future usually were obtained in dreams, hypnosis, meditation, trances, or in a special mental state that all involves the activities of the subconscious. Biological particles, neurotransmitters, and chi obviously play an important role in the process. Such a process might not be able to repeat and can only rely on the psychics' testimony and therefore are not recognized as scientific experiments.

Scientists are too specialized today. For example, physicists ignore the amazing functions of neurotransmitters, and neuroscientists do not notice the physicist meaning of neurotransmitter's velocity. If they are unable to see things from an intricate interconnecttion, they can never create a complete picture of our universe.

Philosophy of Yin, Yang, and Five Elements

Why do I mention the theory of yin, yang, and five elements when I discuss the designated of life events? Life events consisted a series of scenarios that can be visualized. Usually the scenario existed at certain period. They are recognized only when the scenario are been captured.

A mountain, formed by soil and rock, can be seen anytime, and nobody will doubt its existence. However, the scenario of events, composed by vision photon, can only show at a particular time. People would not believe it until it happened, and people do not think it was composed by something because they disappear from our vision some time later. Western science already agreed that some vision phone is involved with the scenario. The Chinese believe the vision phone is something like chi consists of five elements and can be categorized as either yin or yang scale. Before continuing this discussion, I would like to introduce their concepts.

There is an important branch of Chinese philosophy called Taoism. Taoism was founded by Lao-Tze 2,500 years ago. It holds that our universe consists of two worlds—the world of yin and the world of yang. All physical beings belong to yang. Things without physical form and physical life, such as spirits, belong to yin. Entities dwelling in the world of yin are so thin and light that they cannot be detected by a particle detector. For the Western scientist, yin is nothing, or nonexistent. In my belief, they belong to the scale of quantum mechanics.

Taoism has an important concept: *nonbeing and no action*. Taoism believes that everything, including life, will eventually become nonexistent. We thus should not make plans, such as desperately seeking fortune, power, or fame. In other words, since our fate is immutable, we should not override God's will to pursue our own goals but let events happen in their way naturally.

In Chinese, the word *Tao* can be interpreted as "way," "path," or "principle." In his philosophy, Lao-Tze actually explained the origin of our universe. He described an ultimate law that Western scientists are looking for. That law must work in every field and is constant in all circumstances in the universe. Lao-Tze believed yin preexisted yang and is attached to yang. Yin-yang could morph into each other. Shao Kang Jie's great teacher was an important Taoist scholar in Chinese history. Shao himself explained the yin and yang concepts in a wonderful way.

He said that as a nonbeing, yin has no physical size limit and is without a physical lifespan. No physical size limit makes yin exist everywhere, and not having a lifespan makes yin exist forever. In Shao's opinion, yin is more ultimate and crucial than yang. The status of a nonbeing is more important than the status of a being. I believe such a nonbeing is similar to dark matter.

Shao believed:

1. Without the foundation of yin, yang matter could never materialize.

2. Yang matter has a lifespan, its existence is temporary. Only yin exists forever

3. Yin (nothing) and yang (something) can undergo metamorphosis into each other. Nonbeings are manifested when they are shaped. Beings are composed of nonbeings and will disintegrate into nonbeings.

The Chinese people have three words to explain Taoism. They believe all things in our universe can be categorized into three groups: regularity, matter, or chi. Let me interpret them with mo-dern concepts.

Regularity: Rules that govern and run our natural world, such as the sun rising in the east and setting in the west, Newton's law of gravity, Einstein's theory, quantum mechanics, and all the laws that the Western scientific world has recognized.

Matter: Things that can be affected by gravity. Gravity is the crucial force that makes things become manifest visible, tangible, and have mass.

Traditional scientists only recognize and research matter. The Chinese people believe that physics matter is not everything in our universe but are things that can be detected merely. They are just part of our universe, not the only things in our universe.

Chi: The Chinese people consider chi as something other than matter. They use chi (气), a same character, to name energy and air. In their mind, chi, just like energy or air, exists between the boundary of the world of the atom and the subatomic scale. In the quantum world, virtual particles that can jump in or out of existence are similar to Chi. Chi can be either atomic or subatomic particles. Chi might travel faster than light and rejects the pulling power from gravity. As a result, it will lose its mass and weight, existing as a nonatom. When accumulated together and existing as a whole, chi can be detected or can even turn to be matter. That is how yin and yang metamorphosed into each other.

According to Chinese yin-yang theory, all physical creatures, including their physical bodies, carry the yang component (the atom) and the yin component (the chi component). Yin-Yang attach to each other and complement each other as a whole. Connecting them to the human's physics body, yin relates to the chi and soul in our bodies. The yang relates to our physical body, bones, blood, and organs.

An individual's chi is majorly influenced by the universe time trait at the time he was born. Everybody has his own chi component, which is as unique as our DNA or fingerprint. Chi flows between organs inside our bodies *and makes sure they function together properly.* Chi surrounds us like a bulletproof vest and prevents unseen bullets (viruses or bacteria) from attacking us. The Chinese believe that the best way to avoid sickness is to enforce our chi component. They use herbs to nourish chi. Their acupuncture treatments work directly on the channels containing chi. Their chi gong exercises are designed to enforce chi.

The Chinese people are the only human beings who practically deal with Chi. Their medical theory is based on the yin-yang five-element theories. Their acupuncture theory has been practiced for thousands of years, which work in the channel of chi. The way of using a needle to heal illnesses cost almost nothing. Unfortunately, today's hospitals in China give up Chinese medical treatments and adopt Western's testing equipment to maximize their profit.

Western concepts such as aura, subtle or astral bodies are in the same scale as chi. The great Western philosopher René Descartes[4] (1556–1600) believed that the soul was joined to the whole body and disposed of and connected its organs. He said that we have our souls seated in the pineal gland of our brain. He said, "*Spirits are nothing but material bodies of extreme minuteness and that they move very quickly like the particles of the flame which issues from a torch. They never remain at rest in any spot and contain like it a certain very subtle air or wind.*" His idea was similar to the concept of chi (chi also means air in Chinese). However, the most wonderful concept of Descartes's philosophy is ignored even by his disciples.

Chi cannot be detected by a particle detector, and that is why it is not recognized by scientists. Incidentally, I came across a quotation of Einstein's saying. He believed that the earth doesn't pull a stone under any circumstance. Only when the stone gets into a certain field, then gravity could act on it and make it fall. This is why Albert Einstein is great. He did not tell us what things should be in a dominating manner, and he left room for us to do further research as well. He allowed us to raise a question: What do stones look like when they are not in the gravitational field? It could be existing as chi.

Up to today scientists still are unable to detect the graviton and do not understand how it works (a hypothetical elementary particle that mediates the force of gravity). Please allow me to make an assumption here: Graviton existing everywhere does not mean it can function at any circumstance. They might be unable to catch objects that travel faster than light. When graviton is absent, things lose their weight and have their mass turned to zero. Just like what is shown in tunneling and Hawking's radiation, they could not be detected by particle detectors.

Quantum mechanics has confirmed that in tunneling or Hawking's radiation, particles do travel faster than light. They also noticed that when tunneling occurs, particles become invisible. That invisible state is what Chinese called yin. Stephen Hawking also believes that the gravitational field at the event horizon of a black hole is strong enough to turn things into virtual particles and change virtual particles into particles. His theory is similar to the metamorphosis between yin and yang. His baby universe theory actually is similar the concept of yin. In recent years, scientists have come to widely accept that 96 percent of our universe is covered with some unknown matter. That matter cannot be detected by particle detectors and therefore scientists still don't know what it is. However, the existence of such matter is so obvious that scientists couldn't ignore it, and it was named *dark matter.* This dark matter seems to form the background of our universe. It can be the thing that Taoist philosophy means "yin."

Many physicists might hear and remember but don't understand why the founder of quantum mechanics, Niels Bohr, displayed a sign of yin-yang when he was honored by his government. Why did Bohr send his high regard to an Eastern philosophy at that important moment? It is because quantum mechanics theory relates exactly to the metamorphosis of yin and yang. It is regrettable that until today no Western scientists understood Bohr's meaning.

The Chinese yin-yang theory is the ultimate law that West physicists search for. It provides us a whole picture about our universe and explains its origin reasonably. It explains all the supernatural events that have confused us. Shao Kang Jie can even use that to predict an individual's fate and activities. Such an important knowledge system is not known and not accepted by us. We lose its track day by day.

Chi and Healing

With the concept of yin, we can understand the Chinese medical theory more. We can also explain supernatural events that relate to healing. Dealing with subtle bodies can actually affect our physical bodies, and only spirits or our souls can play that kind of role. Below are a few basic healing results that were testified to by many people but were ignored by our scientists.

1. Healers who do not have medical knowledge are able to heal patients just by making psychic readings. Some of them could even perform psychic surgery removing a tumor and leaving no scars on the skin. Psychic healers all frankly admit that their powers are from the spirits. The most well-known psychic surgeon, Jose Pedro Arigo, a Brazilian, claimed that a deceased German surgeon named Dr. Fritz was the healer working through him. In the Philippines, psychic healers got training from their childhood. The method they used the most was practicing meditation. Meditation can shut down our conscious-ness and help us contact spirits subconsciously. A famous psychic healer named Edgar Cayce[5] claimed that his psychic ability was given by a woman sur-rounded by light. Healers usually have no control over the healing result because they did not know what's going on, and some of them even have to surrender themselves to a trance during the time.

2. Patients recovered from hypnotherapy treatment.[8] A Western psychiatrist who practiced traditional medicine, Dr. Brian

Weiss of Yale University, used hypnotherapy to heal long-term illnesses, such as different kinds of strange pains and phobias. He did not understand why recalling past life experiences in hypnosis could cure illnesses that usually cannot be healed by traditional medicine. The reason is when we heal the yin portion of our body and soul, it helps our physical body recover.

3. Meditation, what chi gong theory advocates, can also heal illnesses. If chi gong exercises did not have a positive effect, thousands of people would not voluntarily practice chi gong (such as Falun Gong). Some Western religious meetings also have results of healing. I heard that an Indian religious leader, Benny Hinn, was very successful. I will have a further discussion regarding this important subject later.

All the healing methods I mentioned above have a common characteristic—they work on humanity's chi component (yin). Since humanity's chi component (yin) has a crucial link to its physical bodies (yang), treating one part can benefit the other part. Only spirits can deal with the chi component, and spirits can be either from the dead or the living.

How does the spirit of the living work? I practiced chi gong internal exercises from 1986 to 1991. Once, my son had a high fever that lasted for days. The fever came back every four hours after he took regular medicine. I prayed for help through meditation. I received a message from my chi gong teacher saying that after midnight, my son's fever would disappear. Just as I expected, at midnight my son's fever was gone. I asked my teacher if he knew and if he did something for my son. He said no and told me not to have silly illusions.

During that period, I could divine things simply and easily. When I thought of my friends I could know their habits or feelings that they never mentioned to me. When I asked if they also had that kind of unusual communication with me they all said no. A few times, I automatically wrote things down during meditation.

For example, my hand underlined things in my physiology text book, and that content were questions on the test. My hand circled the homework that I forgot to do, and I never noticed that there was homework. It is amazing that when I asked, "Who was guiding my hand?" My hand automatically wrote down a name—*Wu Yi*. Mr. Wu was my chi gong teacher who didn't know English. How could he circle things in an English textbook?

Worrying that I might go crazy, in 1991, I stopped practicing those chi gong exercises but still kept the question in my mind. On occasion, I heard of an assistant of a famous master who was the founder of the chi gong I practiced. The assistant said that she felt her master visited her at midnight. The master denied the visitation and laughed at the assistant's allusion. The Chinese chi gong practitioner insisted that when he was practicing chi gong, he saw his master and gave him the amazing healing power. However, the master himself was not aware of the visit.

In another case, people report that they were able to heal each other when waiting for treatments from a chi gong master. The illnesses they healed included long-term deafness. All the above information makes me reevaluate the experiences I had before. I concluded that souls not only detach from the dead, they can also detach from the living. Spirits can heal illnesses on the chi component and impact our psychic body.

Again, in order to detach our spirits from our physical bodies, we must go into a trance, hypnosis, or meditation. During that time, psychics have no control of their psychic abilities. They don't know what their subtle bodies do and why the healing results occur.

In ancient China, there was a healing method named *Ling Zi Shu*. Guided by a master, a youth got into a hypnotic state and had his health improved. Not only did his illness automatically disappear, he obtained psychic ability. The Chinese people are very sure that those healing powers are related to spirits. They venerate those spirits because only a sincere and strong wish could communicate them and make them work for us.

Why practicing chi gong can improve our health—doing well, a practitioner might release a lot of gas or yawn a lot. Those reactions make our physical body feel more comfortable. This means that chi gong internal exercises actually affect our parasympathetic nervous system. Illnesses relating to that system are still a challenge to our medical practitioners.

Why does remembering one's previous life experiences in hypnosis result in healing? The soul is still somewhere after the physical body stops functioning. When obtaining reincarnation in a newborn baby, the bad memories from the previous life might still be attached to the soul and that disturbs our physical body. In hypnosis a soul has chances to get rid of the bad experience from its previous life and release its physical body as well.

To summarize my opinion: Humans have subtle bodies and physics bodies (Ying component and Yang component). Healing our subtle bodies can help us recover from physical illness. It can rely on spirits of either the dead or the living. Dealing with the spirits requires strong faith and reverence. We can also get into hypnosis, meditation, or trance to comfort our souls. Chi Gong meditation works on the Chi level and has healing results that traditional medicine does not have.

Chi and Supernatural Events

With the concept of chi, we can also explain supernatural events including Jesus Christ's ability introduced in the Biblical.

Phenomena that are considered supernatural by scientists are as below:

1. Psychokinetic power make objects disappear or become invisible.[16] It captures things from a sealed bottle or from the next door without actually getting there and obtains things from long distances or even from ancient time. In ancient China, psychics could materialize a live fish from the Yellow River or get a flower from Tibet. A bottle of wine can entertain people forever same like Jesus Christ did with five loaves of bread to feed thousands of people. Taoist psychics in ancient China even performed for their emperors. If they were found to be frauds, they were killed.

2. Sharp objects of high temperatures can not harm psychics. They can survive without food or drink for days.[25] They can make their hearts stop and start beating. They might still be alive after being buried for days. It is possible that after being crucified and buried for seven days, Jesus Christ was still resurrected. What the Bible said is the truth, because Jesus Christ had the psychic abilities. We do not have to please scientists to eliminate the most beautiful fundamental part in the Bible. We do not feel upset that the ability that the Jesus

had the Chinese Taoists also had. All we should do is face the fact and find out the truth.

3. People who have psychic power can predict future events, just like Jesus Christ foresaw his betrayal by one of the disciples.

To make all those paranormal events happen, we just need to do one thing: detach the spirit from the physical body. A soul can travel in long distance and travel in a time dimension to get whatever you need. They deal with their yin component and materialize (metamorphose) them later. Detaching from their physical bodies, they don't feel pain when being hurt. They can predict things when traveling in the time dimension, and they can float on the water because they can reject gravity.

Usually the psychics' abilities are derived from the powers beyond the atom. Humans call it occult power, angels, or spirits. Some psychics were born with this ability. I absolutely believe that Jesus Christ had a father from the world beyond the atom which gave him powers that seem supernatural to us.

A famous modern Chinese psychic, Zhang Bao Sheng, could support an object by having strong desire. He never practiced chi gong exercises, nor did he remember how he obtained his physic abilities. He told us that his mother saw a blue light while she was pregnant with him. A famous Israeli psychic, Uri Geller, claimed that when he was five years old, he saw a flash of light that deafened him and gave him a migraine for a few seconds. Since then, metal things around him would automatically change shapes, such as a spoon bent for no reason. Edgar Cayce, a famous psychic healer in the early twentieth century, obtained his ability from a woman surrounded by light.

Humans can also contact spirits and obtain psychic powers through praying. This substantiates why Jesus Christ prayed a lot. I once talked to a group of youths in Hong Kong who practiced Sheng Da, a kind of internal exercise that made them invincible. They weren't afraid of being cut by a knife or being hit by a car. They said that at the critical moment, their medium would help them. The boy who had the experience is a friend of mine. He mentioned things peacefully, and it looks like that is not a big deal for him.

Not only can occult forces cause the supernatural to happen, the willpower of humans holds that characteristic as well. A Chinese chi gong report described the process of telekinesis.[17] When the psychic thinks about the object intensely, the shape of that object would show up in the psychic's brain, and the object would physically disappear simultaneously. When the ectoplasm flows out of the psychic's brain, the object would materialize somewhere randomly.[32] If a psychic moved a watch, the time that the watch shows would be lag behind other watches. The amount of time that the watch lagged was equal to the time that it disappeared. It means that the watch did not exist as a particle when it disappeared and it thus lost its time-keeping functionality.

When I introduced all the supernatural events in my book in 1999, I was worried that those things were too amazing to be accepted until I read Dr. Raymond Buckland's book *The Spirit Book*. I am glad to see that Western psychic researchers have the same records as what I introduced above. They even have pictures proving what actually happens during a séance. It is said that some white substance appearing as steam might be released from any orifice of a medium, their ears, noses, eyes, mouths, nipples, vaginas, or even from their navels. They then form themselves into materialized spirits or part of a spirit (an arm, hand, or face for example). These kinds of spirits were powerful enough to levitate a table or even a piano.

Such a phenomenon is quite important because it relates to the metamorphose process between yin and yang. Again, these processes were ignored by scientists all these years. Humans know the least about our brain—how it functions or what its functions are. Unfortunately, our scientists still insist that phenomena that cannot be explained by their scientific laws do not exist.

How the Chinese Taoists
Practice Their Theory

The Chinese Taoists believe that our world is composed of both yin and yang. The physical world is yang. The subatomic world beyond is yin. They not only have their philosophical theories, they also had psychics to get technical training such as enforcing their psychic ability through practicing meditation by breathing. It is said that when their subtle bodies depart from their physical bodies, they are surrounded by white light from the outer world. Basically, it takes four levels for the human spirit to be levitated.

The first level: Chi flows through the body of the practitioner and dissolves blockages.

The second level: The practitioner has a psychic voyage from their subtle body (the chi component). It detaches from but stays near their physical bodies.

The third level: The subtle body of the Taoist practitioner rejects gravity and can travel long distances and in the time dimension. That is why a psychic can give whatever his audiences request in a psychic performance. Existing as a piece of air, psychics can get into any object—small bottles, paintings, a diamond, or a glass of water. A modern Japanese Taoist practitioner, Gao Teng Chong Yi Lang, confirmed such a possibility through years of practice.

Gao Teng Chong Yi Lang introduced his experiences in a book: *The Chinese Taoist Meditation Way of Being Fairy*. It told how to separate a soul from the physical body. The soul's voyage needs good weather because its energy, or chi, can easily be disturbed by the wind. One day he found that he not only could detach his physical body, he could also enter into a diamond, a picture, or a glass of water. In order to make sure this was not an illusion, he entered into a diamond with his classmate together. It was interesting that those things they saw were about the same. Sometimes they felt it was difficult to remember their experience in the worlds they entered. That means their consciousness were shut down at that moment.

The fourth level: Taoists practitioners can reject gravity, ascend to heaven, and have immortal lives. They can exist as either human or divine spirits (in the subatomic scale). When they scatter and exist as chi, their physical bodies disappear. When they condense themselves, their physical bodies rematerialize. Since they can transfer their existing forms, they can extirpate their physical bodies and avoid physical death. They can also condense their physical bodies and have their lives back. In ancient China, people from many generations claimed that they saw some gods again and again. I believe what they said because these gods were entities that exist as chi.

Basically, supernatural events that relate to Jesus or Mohammed can also be done by ancient Chinese Taoists. In Chinese history, there were eight Taoists who could reach the fourth level and became well-known gods in China. Chinese people venerate their gods and pray for help sometimes. They never consider the god they endorsed is greater than the other gods. They therefore hardly had religious fighting; such as fights between the disciples of Jesus and Mohammed.

Out of all the religions in China, the English scholar Joseph Needham agreed that Taoism was the only system of mysticism, which is not profoundly antiscientific. Taoists not only have a theory similar to quantum mechanics, they also have a great deal of expertise transforming things from atoms to subatomic particles. Unfortunately, their great achievements are considered ridiculous, superstitious, and are treated as fairy tales by the world today.

Psychic Research in the Western World

In Western history, they also had psychics and scholars insist on their research. They recorded many supernatural phenomena seriously and conducted seminars. They even had pictures showing how ectoplasm is released by a medium and how spirits or different kinds of things are materialized in it. It surprises me that no matter how hard they work, they are still rejected by the legitimate scientific world.

In order to make supernatural events occur, psychics or chi gong masters have to deal with their mediums or with their subconscious. Under these conditions we cannot guarantee that psychics work as perfectly as a scientific equipment. Without consideration, scientists might deny the whole of psychic ability even if only one psychic seminar fails.

Scientists dislike psychic power simply because it challenges some traditional scientific premises. They do not know that[13] according to the research of Betty Jo Dobbs and R. S. Westfall, even Isaac Newton wanted to have his system of physics depend upon planetary forces.

Actually, the most important founders of Western science recognized the occult. Johannes Kepler (1571–1630) tried to determine how planets affect human behavior. Newton was a scientist as well as an alchemist. Rene Descartes, founder of geometry, used the word *meditation* to title the most important book he ever wrote. He spent much time practicing meditation.

I believe his knowledge of geometry was obtained during meditation and given by entities about the three-dimensional world. Another great scientist, Einstein, fully believed in the existence of God in his last days. Today, quantum mechanics creates the concept of the virtual particle and opens a door to the occult.

One day, humanity will understand that the higher lives do not have to come from another planet but exist three feet away from us. We could not realize their existence because they are a piece of air in subatomic world.

In the Western world, the most important book, the Bible, mentions a lot of things that sound supernormal for us. I fully recognize the mystical ability of Jesus Christ, including his resurrection. My belief is based on scientific reasons, but not religious reasons. His father is from the other world, and he was supposed to have some psychic powers. I am not sure if he was the Son of God or not. At least I know that he was a real historical person whose psychic ability can prove the existence of God.

Unfortunately, our scientists never try to scientifically explain the psychic ability of Jesus Christ. They do not believe and could not explain the miracles described in the Bible; they leave religion alone. People either simply believe that Jesus Christ was the Son of God or believe that he was a fictional person.

At the beginning of the twenty-first century, a very popular book introduced codes in the Bible. It is said that the most important historical events on earth had been coded in the Bible three thousand years ago. I believe the first Bible was composed by other entities from the subatomic world. In their inertial time frame, historical events on earth are presented all at one time, without past, present, or future. This is the reason the entities who wrote the Bible could foretell historical events on the earth.

Unfortunately, the codes in the Bible were seriously attacked even by religious people. Most religious leaders believe that only they have the right to interpret God, and they don't allow people to prove the existence of God.

Other people attack the Bible Code because they found that codes about historical events were also shown in some other books. We can answer the above accusation in this way: God not only recorded what he previewed in the Bible, he coded what he saw in some other books through other writers' hands as well.

It does not mean the codes in the Bible are not true. It just proves that God is everywhere and God is working hard.

Today, conducting psychic research is still not easy. Scientists, religious people, or politicians constantly and mercilessly discredit psychics. We still have a long way to go.

In the 1980s, a professor from the University of Alaska, Don Elkins, and his partner Carla Ruecker and Jim McCarty wrote a book named *The Law of One*. It researched RA Material, entities from the edge of the universe. As an engineering professor, they tried to make their experiment meet the scientific requirements. They put Carla into a hypnotic trance and allowed RA Material to use her body as a medium to communicate with the authors. Conversations were recorded by a tape recorder hung on Carla's neck. That book was a bestseller then because it contained a lot of enlightenment.

Unfortunately, the research that they performed for a few decades was ignored by our scientific world. Don Elkins died in his fifties and lost his mind before that. For that reason, his book was considered thinking from a crazy guy and was disregarded totally. Exposing himself in the wave from the edge of the universe might result in his going crazy. He sacrificed his life in return for being insulted even more. This was the saddest ending for scientific experiments I have ever heard. I believe one day mankind will give the authors of RA Material the regard that they deserve.

The Law of One answered many questions that have puzzled mankind for years, such as how the pyramids were built and which came first, the egg or chicken. For example, RA Material mentioned that in our universe the world of earth basically has only a "third dimension." Most mankind on the earth were from Mars. Entities lived in Mars destroyed Mars and traveled to the earth in "thought form" (get anywhere instantly by thinking). The Creator adjusted the bodies of apes on earth and let those souls from Mars incarnate in them. This message answers why we *lost track of the evolution between apes and humans. We could not find anything related to a period that was supposed to last for a million years.* It also answers why the climate of Mars is so similar to earth but seems so barren.

When answering questions about the root of thought that created the possibility of disease, RA Material gave an interesting answer. In his opinion, things that threaten humans the most are not disease, but human's greed. He said, "The root cause in this particular society was not so much a bellicose action, but rather the formation of a money system and a very active trading and development of those tendencies towards greed and power; thus, the enslaving of entities by other entities and the misapprehension of the Creator within each entity."[34]

They also remind us that "the beginning entity is one in all innocence oriented" who just had "the need for survival". *It is obvious that seeking extra money and processing trading create all the troubles in our world today.*

When answering the question whether priests represent the Creator—not respecting priests as religious people, usually the RA Material made comments as such: Priests "actually come to the world for learning. The difficulties became apparent . . . as they [priests] were involved not only with learning but became involved with what you would call the governmental structure."[35]

This answer is beyond the box and totally free from conditions. It did not encourage us to listen to the priests. It did not attack or accuse the government structure in the religion organization as well. It simply felt sorry *that those religious leaderships create difficulties for this world.* They used the word *difficulty*, not *disaster*.

Every time when RA Material presented, they greeted the book's authors in the name of Law of One. RA Material told us that in their dimension, all the entities have the same thinking as one and their world thus functions as one. This made me think of the concept of the Lord of one. Humans fight against each other because they believe that only their Lord is the Creator and they do not allow other people to believe in other authority. What a huge misapprehension that the interpretation was switched from "Law of one" to "Lord of one."

RA Material also explains law that the God set up for our three-dimensional world. He said humans are entitled to have free will. Even the Creator has to follow the law and not to interfere with our free will that much. That is why many unfair affairs happened on the earth and God let them go. They let us learn in the process and let us pay for our sin.

When answering question if any great civilization developed in this cycle, RA Material gave an answer that the book's authors never meant to ask and did not understand. This was in 1980s, when China was still a weak country. RA Material said, "In the sense of greatness of technology, there were no great societies during this cycle. There was some advancement among those of Deneb who had chosen to incarnate as a body in what you would call China."[36] This is the only mention related to China in the book. The author simply recorded it and paid no attention. It makes me believe even more that one day the Chinese culture, philosophy and medical theory, should be understood by mankind and would benefit this world a lot more than today. This is one of the reasons I work so hard to promote what I know related to the Chinese culture. This culture is being abandoned by the Chinese due to what their government believes.

A Scientific Experiment Related to Subatomic Particles

Are there any western scientific experiments reflected the metamorphosis of yin and yang chi? I believe there was one—the Philadelphia experiment.[15] In the Second World War, there was a scientific experiment related to gravity in Philadelphia. It is said that Einstein, who spent his late life researching the unified field theory, also joined the experiment. Today the unified field theory is called grand unified theory (GUT). The book of *The Law of One* disclosed that RA material once mentioned the Philadelphia experiment automatically. That made me believe such an experiment did exist. In order to interpret chi on the basis of physics, I am going to discuss phenomena that were shown in this experiment.

The purpose of the Philadelphia experiment was to create an invisible warship. It was theoretically supported by the unified field theory. The theory holds that when a magnetic field is strong enough to bend light, light could cover a warship and make it invisible. In order to change the force of gravity, scientists placed a device on a warship. During the experiment, the warship disappeared for a few seconds and then showed up a few hundred miles away from its original location.

Certain interesting things happened when the warship disappeared:

+ Some people on board the warship burst into flames within a second.
+ A scientist who joined the experiment began to research pyramids.

- People on the warship saw UFOs.
- The survivors from that experiment could go through walls.

Actually, all these unrelated phenomena created an amazing picture of the quantum world. Everything agreed with the regularities of quantum mechanics and happened just as it was supposed to happen. Just because the phenomena happened I believe that there was such an experiment. Those phenomena sound impossible for traditional scientific principles. No one could make up such interesting details when the regularities about quantum mechanics were not even noticed by our scientists. I will discuss these phenomena one at a time in this chapter.

When the warship disappeared, it travels for a few hundred miles in the microsecond. In my opinion, the disappearance of the warship was not caused by bending light. Bending light could not make the warship travel like that. The special device scientists attached to the warship not only bent light, it also eliminated the gravitational force. Losing gravitational force made the warship lose its weight and mass, becoming invisible. Meanwhile, it travel-ed at a terrific speed in an uncertain way. Quantum mechanics has already confirmed that particles might travel faster than the speed of light in tunneling as well as in Hawking's radiation.[9]

Einstein's formula will not work under certain circumstances. When a particle travels faster than light, it could reject the graviton and have its mass turn to zero. In such circumstance $E=mc^2$ totally loses its meaning because $m=0$. Energy generated by the object's terrific motion might add to its mass, but it will never make its mass go up to infinity. There is never a situation of infinity as Einstein's formula predicts.

Just like Newton's laws cannot be applied to objects moving at extremely high speeds, Einstein's formula is not valid for particles traveling faster than the speed of light. The above theories apparently are not the ultimate theories that could interpret all the phenomena in our universe. We therefore should not reject supernatural events to make Newton's laws great. We don't need a Big Bang story to make

Albert Einstein's theory complete as well. There is no such singularity situation he predicted in our universe.

Until now unified field theories only unite three forces—the electromagnetic, strong, and weak force—but does not include the gravitational force because it is the weakest of the four forces. Only Stephen Hawking still gave special prominence to the law that governs gravity. He noticed that *"the attractive force of gravity can win over all the other forces and cause the stars to collapse."*

I believe the gravitational force is a dominant force because it determines the existing form of entities. We can unify the four forces in this way: When the gravitational force is absent, the electromagnetic, the strong, and the weak force will interact in a different way and switch to subatomic particles. Chi is something that can exist as either real or virtual particles. Their switching can change something into nothing.

1. People on that warship saw UFOs when the warship disappeared. This phenomenon proved two things:

   + The warship was not a particle when it was invisible.

   + UFOs are realistic entities but are made of subatomic particles. When the warship disappeared, it existed in the subatomic world that had UFOs. That was why people on the warship could see UFOs.

2. The survivors from the experiment were able to pass through walls. Why did things happen that way? When people on the warship existed as subatomic particles, they carried certain subatomic traits. Such subatomic traits allowed them be able to exist as nothing. When existing as nothing, they can pass through walls without being barricaded.

Actually, all supernormal phenomena such as taking out pills from a sealed bottle, materializing things in the air, removing tumors and leaving no wound on the skin, all are related to the tunneling phenomenon[24] in the quantum world. During tunneling, a particle runs into a wall or barrier that it cannot go through or around; instead it simply disappears and almost instantly reappears on the other side. The scientific world has already confirmed that some types of electrons do this all the time and travel at the speed of light when passing through barriers.

3. Some people on the warship burst into flames within a second.

Physicists contend that particles and antiparticles always annihilate each other, leaving behind only radiation. People in the warship were antiparticles at that moment; therefore, they spontaneously underwent combustion and were annihilated. The US Government refused to confirm the Philadelphia experiment because it was a terrible tragedy that went out of control.

4. When the warship disappeared, people in it either went crazy, burst into flames, or survived. These different consequences agree with the uncertainty principle—an event could have several different outcomes. The survivors' experiences proved that humans could make transformations existing as subatomic particles, not anni-hilating with antiparticles, and then being transformed back to a particle existence.

Here the two discoveries made by Stephen Hawking are proven right and great:

He announced particles do not have to be annihilated with negative particles. Virtual particles can be transformed into real particles in the gravitational field of a black hole.

I considered his opinion amazing because it correctly reflected what happened in the subatomic world and perfect explained the chi gong and psychic phenomena. Chi is something that could exist as either particles or virtual particles. In other words, chi could be something or nothing. Chi gong meditation is one of the ways to reach the transformation. We can also use the above mentioned theory to explain the mystery of the Bermuda Triangle. What happened to those airplanes and ships that disappeared? If they crashed or sank, why did they not leave even one piece of wreckage? The answer is simple. They had been transformed to subatomic particles and stayed in another dimension of our universe.

It could be true that "the end is in sight for theoretical physicists." However, it is not because they have already solved most of the problems of theoretical physics, but because they ignore problems they are supposed to face. They ignored supernatural phenomena which do not agree with Newton's laws. They refuse to research the transformation between particles (yang) and subatomic particles (yin).

5. A scientist who participated in the Philadelphia experiment began to study the pyramids[18] that were built in Egypt a few thousand years ago. I believe he was looking into the possibility of eliminating the gravitational force. It is said a pyramid was about four hundred feet high and built with two and half million limestone blocks. Humans could not achieve this even today, so how could the Egyptians do it then? We must be crazy if we say that extraterrestrials had tools to help the Egyptians to eliminate the gravitational force of the stones. Most scientists would rather avoid the research than being considered crazy.

If there was never a Philadelphia experiment, I will make one here. In order to make Albert Einstein's general relativity theory perfect, our physicists created a Big Bang story. So, why can't we create a Philadelphia experiment to make quantum mechanics beautiful? It is interesting that in the book *The Law of One*, the author disclosed that RA material once mentioned the Philadelphia experiment automatically and said that they were very concerned of that experiment. As a matter of a fact this experiment has more logical details and less nonsense than the Big Bang story, which many of our scientists obsess over. In the next chapter I will discuss it shortly.

Our Universe Originated from Chi, Not the Big Bang

Most physicists tend to believe the universe began with a Big Bang singularity. However, the Chinese people believe that the universe originated from the interaction of Chi. Chi is virtual particles that have a long wave and cannot be detected by a particle detector. The metamorphosis between the yin and yang created our universe. In another word, yin, "*nothing*," originated the universe but not the Big Bang.

According to Dr. Stephen Hawking's *A Brief History of Time*, our physicists still cannot answer some major questions about the Big Bang theory[19] such as the following:

1. How could the temperature of the early universe be so high? It was ten billion degrees at the time of the Big Bang.

2. After the Big Bang, why was the universe so uniform and homogeneous on a large scale, and why was the temperature the same everywhere? How was the heat of that temperature conducted?

3. Why, ten thousand million (ten billion) years after the Big Bang, is the universe still expanding at nearly the critical rate? It is said if one second after the Big Bang the rate of expansion had been smaller by even one part in a hundred thousand million million or hundred quadrillion (one followed by

seventeen zeros), the universe would have collapsed before it ever reached its present size.

4. How could just one Big Bang create so much matter in the universe (articles of one followed by eighty zeroes)?

5. In order to make the Big Bang theory reasonable, physicists made up another inflationary story. They said that when the Big Bang happened, the radius of the universe increased by a million million million million million (one followed by thirty zeros or one nonillion) times in only a fraction of a second.

The Big Bang theory simply states that just before and during the Big Bang, the universe had zero size, was infinitely dense, and had been infinitely hot (and they refused to answer why it was that hot). To avoid answering the question, scientists simply told people that since before the Big Bang no one could exist, it wouldn't make sense to ask who or what caused or created this Big Bang. It is interesting that at this point our theoretical physicists disregard their principle of being precise but provide only a philosophical argument to us.

Let us see why theoretical physicists insist on making up a singularity—a time boundary at the beginning of the universe. They indicate that they "cannot look at the universe by using general relativity without finding a Big Bang." In other words, if there was no Big Bang, Albert Einstein's theory would not be correct in all cases. In order to make general relativity perfect, they create Big Bang stories to agree with an infinity situation. They create stories as well as ignore facts. They simply ignore supernormal events to defend Newton's laws. They forget that even Newton believed in occult forces, and Albert Einstein did not like the idea of a singularity—he preferred to believe that our universe is static all the time. Our scientists all inhabit the infinity building that Einstein built to talk about the story of the Big Bang. If the building collapsed they would have nowhere to go.

Theoretical physicists actually agree that the interference between particles is crucial to the structure of atoms,[22] the basic units of chemistry and biology. They also believe that virtual particles such as photons may not be real particles. Particles "can be created by a very temporary borrowing of energy." "A black hole is strong enough to do astounding things such as turning virtual particles into real particles." My argument is, why can't the interference of virtual particles (chi, nothing, yin) create the particles that eventually originated our universe?

Stephen Hawking said, "When we combine quantum mechanics with general relativity, there seems to be a new possibility that did not arise before: that space and time together might form a finite, four-dimensional space without singularities or boundaries." *I personally believe that instead of a quest for the boundary and singularity of our universe, our scientists should research the boundary of the atom and find out how the transformation performed between the yin and yang occurred.*

A Western theory, the steady state theory,[23] contends that the universe has no beginning and no end. It states that matter is continuously being created by about one particle per cubic kilometer per year and such a low rate actually agrees with observation. The steady state theory also predicted that the average density of galaxies and similar objects should be constant both in space and time. Their first statement seems right; however, the second prediction does not agree with an observation regarding radio waves. Through that observation, physicists concluded that the density of radio waves around us is less frequent than the distant ones—or the sources were more numerous in the past than they are now. For that reason and because of the discovery of microwave radiation emanating from the Big Bang, scientists abandoned the steady state theory.

To support the steady state theory, I explain the problem about frequency in this way.

There are big portions of existence in the universe that are unknown to us, such as dark material. Assume those things have the character of yin—reject the graviton. That material will *tend to escape from gravitational fields.* That is why when we observe them from our gravitational state, we see that radio waves (negative energy) that are distant have a higher density than radio waves near us.

When this kind of material escapes from the gravitational center with the speed of light, they will cause the expansion of our universe just as our observation shows. It can explain why our universe is so huge. It can also explain why our universe does not contract due to gravity. We do not need the explosion from the Big Bang to prevent the contraction of our universe. There is no explosion that can last twenty billion years and is still powerful enough to offset the gravity. It is those yin particles running away from the gravitational center at the speed of light to maintain the balance of our universe, not an explosion.

The above assumption can also explain why the universe is so massive, so uniform, and so homogeneous on such a large scale. When Chi moves away, it creates new space between galaxies. In those spaces, matter is continuously being created.

Taoist yin-yang theory maintains that nonbeings and physical beings can morph into each other. Yin, as the nonbeing, originates the entire physical being of yang, including our physical universe. Yin, things that are without physical size, makes our universe unbounded. Yin also makes our universe without a singularity because Yin has no lifespan. For Taoists, nothing is also something. Before the Big Bang, since the universe contained yin, that nothing was actually something. The concept of yin is very important, and it is similar to things in Stephen Hawking's baby universe.

The concept of yin makes the discussion regarding the origin of the universe seem unnecessary. When discussing the Big Bang theory, our physicists are actually looking for the origin of a *physical universe,* *but* not the origin of our universe. They questioned when these physical things began to exist because in their mind, things must have physical form and a physical lifespan. Again, we are telling them that our universe already existed when nothing was in it because nothing can switch to something.

In *Science and Civilization in China,* English scholar Joseph Needham translated a famous Tao philosopher Chuang Tzu's interpretation about Tao as below:

The Tao has reality and evidence, but no action
and no form. It may be transmitted but cannot be
received. It may be attained but cannot be seen.
It exists by and through itself. It existed before
Heaven and Earth, and indeed for all eternity. It
causes the gods to be divine and the world to be
produced. It is above the zenith, but it is not high.
It is beneath the nadir but it is not low. Though
prior to heaven and earth it is not ancient. Though
older than the most ancient, it is not old.

The above interpretation seems like speculative philosophy. It actually contains an important meaning in physics. Chuang Tzu disregarded the traditional concepts of time and space and elevated things to a higher level. Near-death experiences and meditation experiences disclose that there is no difference between the past, present, and future in the other world. That mean time does not exist; there is no difference between one second and one year. Space does not exist as well. They can be in many places at the same time and can be at anywhere at any time by just making a wish. *In my opinion, no time interval means that the universe just has no beginning and no end. No space can mean our universe has no boundaries. Our research about the origination of our universe has no any meaning.*

Shao Kang Jie believed that time passes in cycle after cycle. His calendar considers 129,600 years as one cycle. During a cycle, things are created and developed, then they decay and die. According to his calendar, we are about in the year of seventy thousand of our cycle. After this cycle ends, another cycle will start.

Eternity and harmony are two important concepts in the Chinese philosophy. The basic principle of their five-element theory is harmony. This theory is similar to the Pythagorean and Neoplatonic theories. If there is a complete unified theory that covers everything in the universe, I believe this theory should relate to harmony, transmigration, and yin-yang theory, but not to the concept of infinity. No force can reach infinity in our universe because our universe always has different forces to offset each other to maintain its balance.

In summary, chi can transform from particles to subatomic particles. Since subatomic particles always move away from a gravitational field, it prevents the contraction of our universe due to gravity. Chi is being and nonbeing. Starting from a subatomic scale, chi interacts and originates particles that eventually form our world. There is no singularity or boundary in our universe but the boundary of the atom and the transmigration of yin and yang.

Stephen Hawking once felt sorry that today's philosophers have not been able to keep up with the advances of scientific theory. He noticed that in the eighteenth century, philosophers considered the totality of human knowledge, including science, to be their field, and discussed questions such as if the universe has a beginning. I understand Dr. Hawking's feelings. I don't know if he considered that the philosophy of yin-yang actually gives enlightenment to our scientists today.

Events Are Created by Chi
and Time Has Its Traits

What are events? Scientists believe that an event has something to do with the speed of light. According to their logic, if our world has particles that travel faster than the speed of light, we would be able to envision people born even before their parents. Our scientists worry that such a disorder would mess up the sequences of events themselves. They, including Albert Einstein, set up a rule saying in our universe there is no particle that travels faster than the speed of light. Actually, the speed of light has nothing to do with the occurrence of events. It does not determine the order in which events happen as well. We can view past or future events by getting to the related range of time but are unable to change them. People's near-death experiences verified to us that when they reviewed he past events they could not interfere with them.

If the speed of light has nothing to do with the occurrence of events, then what actually determines the happening of events? First, let us see how events happen and how visions are obtained, according to the zero point field version of physics.[28] The zero point field embraces a plethora of virtual particles (long-range forces that cannot be detected by particle detectors), and some of them are virtual photons. Virtual photons are particles of electromagnetic energy that essentially exert forces on the back of our eyes. Our eyes and brain then interpret these forces as vision and events. Chi and virtual particles both are something that could not be detected by a particle detector.

In other words, virtual photons in different traits of time compose different scenarios. Their existence obviously relates to the world of the quantum. Without the interaction of those time traits and virtual photons, we could not envision the related scenarios. The time traits and virtual photons are influenced by the rotation of the planets and have a tight connection with each other.

Why do events look like a coincidence for us? It is be-cause only at a particular moment virtual photon carries certain traits that are able to convey certain visions, not before or after that. Such traits fill in the universe and change ac-cording to the movement of the planets. When the traits of time change, the scenario that we envision disappears. How-ever, it does not mean that the scenario disappeared forever. Because events are always in some time dimensions that when psychics enter the related trait of time, the scenarios are being captured.

It is just like a mountain has already existed somewhere in the three-dimensional world. Why should I introduce the concepts of Chi when I discuss the predestination of life events? It is because I believe just like a mountain is created by rocks, the scenario of events are composed by chi. They are always somewhere, which allowed psychics to preview and predict them.

To sum up this chapter, time, not only as Albert Einstein said, has not only a related interval, it also has related traits. I would name them imaginary elements, a concept that is similar to Stephen Hawking's imaginary time. The traits of time change every five minutes according to the movement of the planets and can interact with the chemical substances in our brains. The interactions determine what we see, how we think, and the decisions we make. This is how the traits of time, or chi, influence human behavior and cause events to occur. This is why we say that chi creates events.

We cannot measure the traits of time, but it does not mean they do not exist. We can know their existence from the outcome of an event. Just like annihilation can prove the existence of antiparticles, a falling apple can prove the existence of the graviton.

How Chi Influences
Our Life and Fate

According to Einstein's relativity, different time frames might exist in our universe. If a message could be transferred between the different time frames, predicting future events become possible. I meanwhile believe the speed of neurotransmitters can be faster than light. That is why many supernatural events are involved with human's psychic ability.

Next I am going to discuss my original topic—why life events are predestined and why Shao Kang Jie could predict future events based on knowledge—hexagrams and the interaction of chi.

Our lives are composed by different experiences that carry sceneries. They look like they happen by coincidence, but they are not. Since some people can preview sceneries in the future, we said that the scenery is already somewhere. It is determined by the interaction of the traits of time and our biochemical substances that related to our aura (trait of our birth time). Those interactions determine our fate—how?

We all agreed that life is tremendously determined by the decisions we made for it. Surrounded by harmonious interactions we tend to make good judgments and right decisions. Surrounded by harmonious interactions we can successfully attract benefactors and avoid enemies.

A harmonious interaction can give us good health to finish what we want to do. Aura, just like our armor, can resist invasions from viruses. By instinct criminals might attack the victim whose aura is weak and avoid people who have strong energy.

The interactions of chi majorly influence our instinct. Their outcome determines how we think and what we do. I believe the scenery we see is created by the virtual photons, changing that can change what we see. That was why a psychic could make someone believe a piece of paper was a train ticket. People might have different perceptions or reactions regarding the same event. What determines their decision? Many times they make decisions based on instincts which connect to their biochemical substances rather than based on their life backgrounds. I believe that the interaction of cosmos chi and our birth time traits can impact the biochemical substances in our brain and cause decisions we make. Those signals impact our fate by influencing our perceptions and our decisions.

It always happens that well-educated people become losers in their lives because they fall in love with the wrong person. A person who did not finish school makes right choices and gets lifelong benefits, such as buying a lotto ticket. Many time those decisions were made by their instincts within a second.

How do instincts affect someone's life? Below is a report in *Digest* about how a person survived from a serious car accident. The traffic congestion was very bad. As a passerby, a doctor took care of the injured and insisted to transport him by a helicopter. Without his suggestion the injured would have died.

What impressed me the most was that the doctor hardly drove on that road all these years. That day, an idea flashed in his brain and made him turn his car to the accident scene. Without that flashing idea the story would have a different ending.

This explains what fate is. How does a small idea or instinct totally change someone's life? Instincts are affected by the traits of time. It looks like the doctor's aura has some elements that benefit the injured. The doctor's accidental decision contained predestined factors as well. It could be the injured did not deserve death yet; God sent a signal to the doctor and let him help the injured. The departed family members of the injured created the doctor's instinct and put him at the scene. Such varied endings agree with the uncertainty principle and relate to the traits of time. Only God or spirits can change events by changing the traits of visual photons and eventually change the ending of events. The traits of time are imaginary elements—chi or yin.

Why Events Are Predestined and How to Predict Them

I have mentioned that the interaction of the birth time trait (aura) and the changing universe time trait influence our fate. Now, I am going to answer why from the same universe time traits someone has good luck and someone has bad luck. We all assume that car accidents are caused by a driver's negligence or mechanical problems. My question is, Why did an accident happen at that particular time, in that particular place, and to that particular person but not in some other combination? The answer lies between the time traits (determined by rotation of the planets) and the individual's birth time trait that gives the person an aura. We might never have a precise answer about how planets influence an individual's destiny when so much remains unknown in our vast universe. However, we should not stop the research since such influences do exist.

We all agree that the impacts created by the rotation of planets tremendously influence the earth. A small moon in the distant sky controls the tides. The distance between the earth and sun makes plants bloom or wilt. As biological beings on earth, there is no way to avoid the impact the planets apply on us. They are not only influencing the weather, they also affect our moods, our judgments, and our decisions by impacting our birth time traits, auras. Why, under the same trait of time, does someone have good luck and others bad luck? It all relates to the interaction of the five elements that are buried in the trait of time.

Cosmic time traits penetrated into our bodies at the time we were born and exists as our aura. They are composed of five elements that might back up or overcome each other. The net results caused by their interaction influences us every minute in our life. Cosmic time traits continue to change according to the movements of the planets and their impact on our aura, thus they are changing every minute. With the interaction between the five elements, a harmonic outcome will give us good luck and help us make right decisions. A conflicted impact will cause bad luck for us. *Since universe time traits change every five minutes, our birth time trait that created our aura is different. It is as identical as our DNA or fingerprints. People have different luck in the same universe time trait because when their aura, birth time traits, interact with the universe time traits, the outcome is different.*

The Chinese believe chi has five elements—metal, wood, water, fire, and earth. These elements create the trait of time. The outcome of their interactions directly impacts our fate. For predicting an individual's life, we have to know the interaction between his birth time trait (aura) and the changing universal time traits. That is why Chinese astrology always requires two kinds of data:

1. It needs the individual's birth time to figure its birth time trait and determine the five elements his aura consisted of.

2. Calendars or an entire array of planetary charts help them calculate the cosmic traits at any particular time. That way they can predict the fate that an individual has in that particular time.

Traditionally the Chinese did not use numbers to name years like the Western calendar does today. They have twenty-two characters that are linked to five elements, metal, wood, water, fire, and earth. The twenty-two characters create sixty permutations, and they then use the sixty permutations to name the year. They even use that to name the months, days, and every two hours. In that way we can calculate the traits of time for every two hours. Combining with the permutation of year, month, and day, there are more than one million different permutations to express the traits of time every two hours. They then predict our fortune basing on the interactions of the five elements that relate to our aura and the universal chi.

In Chinese, both *air* and *energy* are named by the same character chi (气). They are both seething[6] in our universe and cannot be detected. The Chinese people believe that chi in the universe has five different traits: metal, wood, water, fire, and earth. The traits are changing every five minutes according to the rotations of the planets. They tie up with time and become the trait of time. Something seething in the air and cannot be detected—looks like it is in the subatomic scale and relates to the world of the quantum. The Chinese use five elements to interpret the birth time trait and the changing universal time trait.

The Chinese calendar contains information that is not on the other calendars. It lists the five elements in the cosmic world for each day and allows us to figure the time traits up to every two hours. (Shao Kang Jie can figure the time trait of every five minutes.) The theory of Chinese astrology is mature and complete. It involves five element theory, I-Ching hexagrams, and the planets' array. For them, predicting an individual's fortune is basing on knowledge, but not psychic power.

Today, successful Western psychics did challenge the traditional scientific principles in some way. Their predictions remind us that there are still some things too amazing to be explained by the existing scientific laws. However, since they did not have a whole system or formula to work with they can just predict things by chance. They cannot meet what the scientists needs.

Shao Kang Jie was the one who predicted things by using hexagrams and formula. Based on the birth minute of a person, he could list the birth years of that person's family members. His book said that I should have a husband twelve years younger than me. Since he knew what would happen he must also know why that happened. Unfortunately, we lost track of his whole system, and he was hardly known even by the Chinese today.

Factors That Might
Change Life Events

In real life, it always happens that things do not occur like the predictions said. We also face questions such as why someone was able to be born at a "lucky" time and the others were not. Why are people born at about the same time and have different fates? The answer is because there are other factors that could change the interaction of chi and make events happen in uncertain ways. God, spirits, and events exist in the same dimension which has virtual photons. They can interfere with events by changing those photons. They can send signals to our brain to change our decisions. They are always watching us; they make us pay for our sins and reward us for the charity we do.

A birth time trait also is connected to our karma in the previous life and set by God as well. The birth time trait made things happen and predetermined our life. God also rewards or punishes what we did and changes our destinies in some way. Because they interfere, miracles happen and fate looks unpredictable.

A spiritual entity (including God) can alter events by changing the traits of virtual particles. Spirits exist in the same dimension as events. They, just like us, exist in the same world as physical matter. In the physical world we can easily make, move, or break tables. However, spirits could make incredible events happen at a table, such as causing enemies to fall in love, causing someone who is illiterate to create beautiful poetry, or causing someone to get the hiccups. Praying can communicate with spirits and cause miracles to happen. In other words, God and spirits interfering might change the outcome of events.

Not only the spirit or God, the living chi component can change the interactions of chi and eventually change the consequences of events. Interaction between people's aura also influences our fate. This could explain the butterfly effect, a small factor that changed history. In the car accident previously mentioned, the doctor's aura obviously combined well with the aura of the victim. He therefore could get to the scene of the accident and play an important role in saving the person's life. The whole thing proved predestination.

Why do people who are born in the same year, month, day, hour, minute, and places have different lives? Can we change our fate? Our answer is yes! I have mentioned previously that our fates are also influenced by our karma. Karma is accumulated from our past lives, our ancestors, or what we do in our present life. So we can change fate by maintaining a good karma. Below is a famous history in ancient Chinese:

Scholar Yuan Liao Fan used *Tie Ban Shen Suan* to predict his whole life. It listed his scores in all the exams he took, saying that he was ranked fourteenth in the county's officer enrollment exam, ranked seventy-second in the province exam, and ranked ninth on another exam. Things all came out like what it said. It also said in a certain year he would be selected as an officer in Sichuan and he would quit the job three years later. That also came true. Once, something happened to delay his promotion until a few years later like what Shao Kang Jie predicted.

Shao Kang Jie also said that he would die on August 14 when he was fifty-three years old. He could not have children all his life. Since everything happened like what Shao predicted, Yuan accepted that life was predetermined. He made no plan and had no desire for his future.

One day Yuan met a monk and had meditated with him for four days in a row. The monk could tell that Yuan did not have any plan for his life and asked him why. Yuan answered, "Life is predestined and cannot be changed anyway." The monk said that usually people's fates were impacted by the magnetic field. However, power beyond us can change our destiny for the extremely good or bad behaviors we did. Therefore, helping others could even-tually bring good luck to a person.

Since then Yuan did charity every single day and recorded them carefully. After doing one thousand good deeds, he had a son. During that period, he reduced the taxes as a governor of an area. In a dream he was told that the policy he carried out equaled ten thousand good deeds because it actually benefited thousands of people. That means a person who practices a wicked policy, such as launching a war, could be considered committing crimes ten thousand times. For the good deeds Yuan did, he lived almost twenty years longer than Shao's predictions.

On the whole, factors I mentioned previously—karma, God, spirit, our auras—all influence our fates. Calculating the interactions of chi is not like solving a math equation, but with some uncertainty. One event has a few possible outcomes, and the total sum is unchanged unless you did something special and touch entities in the other world.

As what I said previously, God, spirits, and our auras can interrupt the interaction of chi and make events happen beyond predestination. However, since such interfering rarely happens, the influence of the planets are still dominant in our fate. That means, based on planetary movement, we still should be able to predict an individual's fate at a certain point.

In here, being predestined can mean that a soldier has no way to become a professor or that a doctor could not play in an NBA basketball team. Someone could be destined to get rich by finishing his college degree and having a good job or make money from his own business directly and do not need an academic degree.

Predetermined also means the sum of positive and negative things we have are fixed in our life. For example, someone had bad luck in a particular year. After losing a large amount of money, he is able to survive from a car accident. It is because most of his bad luck already impacted him and his financial situation. Someone died soon after winning the lotto because the fortune he gained is more than he deserved.

Data below recorded experience after some people won the lotto. It can more or less prove what I mean.

In the town of Acadia, Michigan, a forty-three-year-old man died from a heart attack twenty months after he won a big prize in the lotto. He died from a health condition.

Another man, Jack Whittaker, won three hundred million dollars in Powerball. He meant to give that money to his granddaughter, but she died from a drug overdose at the age of seventeen years. After he got that money, his wife asked for a divorce and his other daughter had cancer. Besides that, since he won the money, he had 460 court cases. He was very unhappy and wished that he never won the Powerball prize.

In 2001, Thomas Turnour from Victorville won ten million dollars in the Super Lotto. On August 15, 2008, he got a seventeen-year sentence in San Bernardino. He drove a car while intoxicated and caused the deaths of three people. The lotto winner paid almost all his money in the legal fees before going to jail.

I don't mean everybody who won the lotto had a sad ending. I noticed that in the program of HGTV some lotto winners did have a strong trait showing in their aura. I just mean when the money we received is more than our birth time frame (aura) could sustain, bad luck will appear to cancel the good things out and make the totals we deserve unchanged. In other words, when we are extremely bene-fited by something, we would lose other things somewhere else.

It could happen that twins have totally different lives even though their birth minutes are close. For example, my uncles were twins. They both worked for the Hong Kong government, had good incomes, and had a nice housing allowance. The older twin had four children; two were medical doctors, one had a PhD degree, and one was a successful businessman. However, the younger twin had no children at all. In these cases, I would consider the twins to be one person. When one had all the good luck, there will be no good luck left for the other. They died in the same year. Their money both was taken by unrelated people and did not go to their children or adopted child.

The Meaning of Researching Predestine

Questions might be raised here: If the future of one's life is unpredictable in some way, what is the point of having foreknowledge? It is true that we can also do what we are supposed to do without preknowing things in the future. However, there is nothing wrong to know as well. We can use that as a reference to plan our life, like continue building up businesses or go back to school for a degree. We can prepare in our minds for negative things such as divorce or surgery.

Researching the predestination of life events and researching chi not only has an academic meaning, it can benefit our society as well.

With the concept of chi, we can recognize the result of psychic healing, and it's when we depend on the spirit's healing, the yin portion of our bodies, that we can actually heal illness in our physical bodies.

With the concept of birth time traits (aura), we can understand better. Sometimes criminals committing crimes at the moment is due to the results of the interaction of time traits. It can balance or reform by referring the time element they need. The way is to match people's aura by studying the five elements shown in their birthday chart.

It provides a new basis for our life goals. It has no meaning to just seek for fortune. Instead we should live in a balanced way, with health and happiness. Because the sum of the positive things they can obtain is the same in their lives anyway, capturing something more will lose the other things eventually.

Using the concepts of chi and yin, we will try to use a medium, but not a spaceship, to communicate with higher beings. We know they are not in the other star but are three feet away from us. We must behave ourselves because some powerful entities are monitoring us.

Most of all we should know the truth about our lives. I am announcing here that the Chinese astronomer Shao Kang Jie was able to predict human behaviors by formulas. He accurately predicted a person's career, personality, and marriage status. He could even calculate the birth years of a person's direct family members. His achievement proved that our lives are predetermined. The theory he used included the Chinese yin-yang theory, the I-Ching hexagrams, and the five-element theory. It is sad that the calendar he set up his whole life was not understood by an emperor at his age. He was well-known by people then, but his name and his system were hardly known by even the Chinese today.

Stephen Hawking once commented, "*The European four elements theory was simple enough to qualify as one, but since it did not make any definite prediction, it 'does not satisfy the requirements of a good theory.*'" He also said, "We have had little success in predicting human behavior from mathematical equations." In his later life he admitted that it is very difficult to predict future events.

Shao Kang Jie was the one who used five elements to predict people's lives in a precise way, such as declaring that a person born at my birth time will have a husband twelve years younger.

Stephen Hawking also said, "Most scientists have been too occupied with the development of new theories that describe what the universe is than to ask the question why?" Mr. Shao Kang Jie was the person who could answer the question "why?" without knowing why. He would not be able to create a formula and use it to predict mankind's behavior. Mr. Shao's achievement was greater than Isaac Newton and Albert Einstein and Stephen Hawking. It is a shame that he remains unknown by even the Chinese and of course he was impossible to be recognized by the scientists of today's world.

Traditional Western scientists do not even realize that important events in our lives are predetermined. They cannot catch what Mr. Shao Kang Jie has achieved. Mr. Shao Kang Jie is still way ahead of us. For that reason I wrote and promote this book.

In some way, Chinese culture is much more scientific than what we knew. Chinese medical theory, chi gong (气功) theory, yin-yang five-element theories, I-Ching theory, Fung Shuei (风水) theory, and the theory of future prediction are all related to the world beyond the atom, Yin. The whole set of culture was inherited from our ancestors in hundreds of years but was considered ridiculous by this world today. In their mind the Chinese only had four inventions in history—paper, the compass, gunpowder, and printing.

Dr. Stephen Hawking, one of the most respected physicists after Einstein, explained why scientists want to learn the origins of the universe. He said that "*since the dawn of civilization, people have not been content to see events as unconnected and inexplicable. Humanity's deepest desire for knowledge is justification enough for our continuing quest. And our goal is nothing less than a complete description of the universe we live in.*" That is precisely the reason for discussing the concept of predestination.

Steven Hawking's statement is beautiful. Unfortunately, our scientists did not really practice it. For protecting the scientific laws that they have faith in, they choose to ignore supernatural events. For proof of Einstein's infinite situation, they make up a Big Bang story. How can they get a full picture of our universe when they act so conservatively, diminutively, and authoritatively? At this moment we do not need an "air of legitimacy" that they gave to Professor Joseph Rhines mercifully. We do need the air with freedom. They can enjoy their legitimate scientific world and please each other as long as they are not blocking our path to the truth.

Part Two

Data

I Witnessed How Shao's
Predictions Work

Learning about Shao Kang Jie

The first time I heard about Shao Kang Jie was in 1974, when I worked in a bookstore. One day, a customer asked if we sold a book with the title of *Tie Ban Shen Suan*, written by Shao Kang Jie. He said having that book could help him to win the Nobel Prize, and I though he lost his mind at the moment. Later I found out he had novels published in the newspaper. He was not that crazy as I thought. He did not tell me why the book was so important to him. However, the book *Tie Ban Shen Suan* caught my attention since then. In Chinese, *Tie* means "iron" (not flexible). *Ban* means "abacus," *Shen* means "amazing," and *Suan* means "calculation."

A few months later, my friend visited me in the bookstore. He had an art degree from a Canadian college, and like most of the artists, he tended to do things that were against set traditions. He felt proud of his Western educational background and considered Chinese culture superstitious. That day he acted like he was drunk as he mentioned *Tie Ban Shen Suan* to me. He said, "Believe it or not, everything is predestined and has already been printed in a book nine hundred years ago. The book said that my friend should have a wife eight years younger than him, and it was true."

I was impressed by what he introduced but had no desire to find out what the book said about me. For doing that I had to spend my four months' worth of salary and wait in line for one year because during that time only one person knows how to use that book in Hong Kong. A few years after that, one day I walked in the street and was blocked by an advertisement saying, "Read you future in *Tie Ban Shen Suan*—cost only $50." Inside a messy room a fortuneteller agreed to charge me only thirty dollars due to my bargaining. I did not know if his predictions were accurate and decided to pay as less as I can. That fortune teller became my master and business partner since then till I immigrated to the United State. Many years after he still remembered how I bargained, and I laughed at that poor advertisement board placed in the sidewalk.

Shao's Predictions about My Family

Basing on my birth time, the fortuneteller started to verify the minute that I was born. I only knew that I was born in the morning at about eight in the morning. The first few sentences the book pulled out did not sound right for my case until it said, "Born at this moment the individual's parents are still alive." That was my case, but it seemed too general because most people would have their parents alive at the age of twenty-six years.

Based on that birth minute, the next sentence said that my mother was a pure, virtuous, and cautious woman who always followed rules. That sounded correct but still far from amazing. I was surprised by the third sentence, which summarized my father's life. It said, "He treated people honestly, and people humiliated him in return." The sentence looked like they made no sense, but for me the description was very accurate. My father was a Chinese medical doctor. He needed to take care of a few dozen patients each day and got twenty dollars salary per month. Still people mistreated him because he came from a capitalist family in Hong Kong. People might get humiliated accidentally in their life, but my father must reform his thought in the long run, criticizing himself and accepting people's attacking. People did it for proof that they love the government but not a capitalist literature. I could not help tearing when I read that comment. I wrote every day as a news editor, yet I could not use a better sentence to describe my father's life in China than what Shao Kang Jie did.

The book then said that my father was stuck in a well and he would get out of there eventually. In 1949, when people ran away from the Communist party, my father gave up good job in Hong Kong and moved back to Red China to service them. The process was just like falling into a well. Shao Kang Jie did not say my father was being jailed. As a matter of fact, the government never really jailed my father. They just considered him a political deviant and let people attack him in every political movement. Shao mentioned my father's life very accurately.

I noticed later that Tie Ban Shen Suan did had particular descriptions for people who were convicted. Just because he had his own business, my friend's father was jailed for twenty years. Shao said, "It was a tragedy that this man had to spend his life in jail."

The prediction said that my father would get out of the well eventually. When I got that sentence, I thought that meant after the Cultural Revolution, my father would be left alone and everything would be okay again. I did not expect that my father would be able to immigrate to the United States in 1978. He not only got rid of those troubles but got out of that well.

The predictions about my siblings said that someone always held her cash box and kept every penny. My teacher told me that the comment could be about any of my parents' children, including myself. I did not pay attention to that kind of description because it was exaggerated and was too common. Fifteen years after that, I requested a reading for my husband. The same sentence showed up in his record. My teacher said that should mean my teller job in the bank—I had to count my cash box every day and made sure no any penny was shorted.

One Sentence Covered Six Generations

A sentence said that, "My ancestor's conglomerate dissolved, the foundation of my son and grandsons has more than they need." My father was a poor herbalist in China, and he never owned a business. My grandfather filed for bankruptcy when he was twenty-seven years old. All his money was from his father, and he never built up any business. The businesses that the book mentioned must belong to my great-grandfather.

In the museums of Canton and in Chinese high school textbooks, my great-grandfather Chan Qi Yuan (陈启源) was recognized as the first capitalist in China and was the most important person in the Chinese textile industry. He invented a steam machine to separate silk from the chrysalis of the silkworm. He had businesses in Hong Kong, Vietnam, Macao, and Canton during those years. During the eighteenth century, he had two steamships that exported silk and tea, products of his own factories, overseas.

The first half sentence related to my great-grandfather, and from him to me there are four generations. Before the 1900s, China hardly had *conglomerates* or *foundations*, words that are in Shao's predictions regarding my fate. However, since those words do correctly categorize my great-grandfather's business, I believe that Shao's statement related to my son and grandson should also be correct. My descendants will have more than they need. My son has a very rich Jewish grandfather who was a successful businessman and had CPA practicing in New York for fifty years. Theoretically, he should have a trust fund for my son.

In the predictions related to my son, a sentence said that following the track, my son will get things prepared for him and I-Ching's calculation should be precise. In 2015, my son's grandfather passed away, and all his nine-million-dollar estate were stolen by the nieces of his third wife. I filed a court case against them, and for four years, no supreme courts wanted to get involved in it. I am going to bring them to the criminal court now because even the attorney general said they were criminals. I felt that every crucial moment I was guided by a power to continue my fighting. I even believe that being allowed by his Jew's God, the grandpa will come back as my grandchildren to control his money. They drove me to fight hard. However, even though without the grandpa's estate, I had my own properties, over two million dollars, for my son and grandson. I did not expect that I would run things so well twenty years ago when I wrote this book.

Viewing Things from Different Angles

The difference Shao's predictions about my father and my uncles were interesting. About my uncles, he said, "Your ancestor built up the business and you spent all the funds. Your rich life is over." When I read that comment, I disagreed with it. It was my grandfather who made my great-grandfather's business bankrupt, not my uncles. My uncles did inherit a building in a very good neighborhood, but with only four floors. Each of them had half of an apartment worth about a few thousand US dollars then. Compared with the assets that my grandfather lost, it was almost nothing. Therefore, accusing my uncles of using up the ancestor's fund seemed unfair.

After a few years I understood what Shao meant. Because of the location today, that building is now worth a few million US dollars, no longer one hundred thousand US dollars. My uncles sold out their inheritance in 1975 before the real estate market went up in Hong Kong. It was very interesting that the book did not say my father used up his ancestors' fund. It only said that *"it is unbelievable that such a big business ended up that way."* It was true that my father was in China and he did not get any inheritance from his ancestor.

Shao's book predicted the fate of my friend and his two sisters. Three of them had the same father but got different comments, yet all were amazingly accurate. My friend himself had to work as a barber apprentice to make a living when he was ten years old. His father never supported him financially. The prediction described his early life this way, "It is just like drinking ice water in cold winters, you would remember every drop of the water that you swallowed." His two sisters got support from their father. In one of his sister's charts, Shao said her father *"traveled a lot in his life,"* and regarding another sister's father, Shao said, "His *disciples were everywhere.*" It happened that his father traveled all over in China for almost thirty years, and as a barber he taught apprentices all his life. There were more than a hundred people who learned from his father and worked all over the country.

Shao's Other Predictions That I Knew

Since 1978 Mr. Tong taught me various things about the knowledge of astrology except Shao's formulas. I paid rent for his office and shared his profit. I also wrote down Shao's predictions for his clients that gave me a lot of chances to see how amazing Shao was. Our business relationship ended in 1984 when I immigrated to the United States.

During those years I noticed that Shao's theory predicted things in accurate and beautiful ways. One sentence might cover a lot of meaning. For example, the sentence about my personality said that I am a "freely romantic and excellent person who always changes her mind." When my friends heard it, they all laughed and said that was amazing. I have to admit that I couldn't introduce myself as accurately as Shao did.

The book had different descriptions for the similar jobs that were on different levels. My friend's father is a bookkeeper; the book said that he is a person who would not like to see a small error in his account. I once was a cashier. The book said that I kept a cash box carefully and don't want to lose even a penny. My son's grandfather was a Jewish CPA. The book said that "for this man, there are figures inside figures. Every decision he made was based on calculation."

The book has three different descriptions regarding the career of astrologers. A blind man got a sentence in the book saying that "this man could know future events by throwing three coins." The blind man was so surprised that he showed us his business card to prove that he was a professional fortune-teller. He set up I-Ching hexagrams by throwing three coins, and from the hexagrams he made predictions.

Another blind fortune-teller, Chan Wei Ming, visited my teacher with a few famous astrologers in Hong Kong. They wanted to see how much my teacher knew about *Tie Ban Shen Suan* and wanted to see how amazingly the book worked. According to the birth time Chan presented, no sentence we pulled out fit his case. For example, the book said that people born at that quarter must *had four brothers who are from three different mothers*. Chan did have three mothers but did not have four brothers. I lost my patience at that moment and asked

Chan how come three mothers did not have four sons in those days. I worried that they were playing games with us. My teacher calmed me down and finally found out that Chan's birth time was a little bit later than what he claimed because it was summertime when he was born.

After his birth minute was determined, every sentence my teacher pulled out about Chan was correct, such as Chan was able to communicate with spirits. Chan did not know anything about Yi Jing hexagrams, yet he could tell things with amazing accuracy. For example, he could describe what his clients' homes look like without actually going there. People usually got up at 4:00 a.m. to wait in the line in order to have a psychic reading from him. His predictions seemed related to spirits, but no one could prove that. Shao said it was positive and printed his statement in a book. Everybody was surprised that day.

Up to today, I am not sure of my career in my life even though I worked as an accountant all these years. Shao's book mentions my husband's wife.

It said that *"by using a pen made of metal she wrote down the good news and bad news in our world. [A pen made of metal here has the meaning of predicting definitely.] By throwing three coins she could predict events that only God knows."* Today, Chinese fortune-tellers hardly write things down, instead they use tape to record what they said. I was a newspaper editor in my twenties and that gave me a habit of writing things down when I read horoscopes. I did know how to set up hexagrams by throwing coins. However, I disagree that I know things that only God knows. I could never predict things like Shao Kang Jie did. I don't think I could figure Shao's formula. I don't study hard, and I can never meet the level Shao said.

Shao's book was able to define the difference between three of us. When I read charts, I use pens and I know how to throw coins. The first blind man, Chan, only used coins because he could not see and write. The second blind man had no knowledge about hexagrams. He didn't use pens or coins but was able to communicate with spirits. Shao's descriptions didn't mix up anything and mentioned accurately about what we could do. These kinds of predictions are impossible to be made by chance.

The book not only described peoples' traits, occupations, family background, and their life experiences, it also described scenarios of events. The case that my friend's father died with his eyes open was the scenario of a deathbed. There was another prediction related to this scenario. It said that "when hair in your armpit falls off something bad would happen." The first time I saw the sentence it was related to a female client in Hong Kong. I was curious and asked her if the sentence had some particular meaning. She told me that in one year right after hair in her armpit fell off, her husband died.

One of my friends also had the same sentence in his marriage column. For more than ten years we did not know its exact meaning. In 1993, my friend's wife had surgery on her breast. She told me that when a nurse was shaving the hair in her armpit, she remembered Shao's prediction, and she believed that she had cancer. The result later confirmed that the tumor she had contained cancer cells.

Shao's prediction was too amazing to be believed. Someone said that my teacher collected information when he verified the minute of birth for his clients, and based on this information my teacher pulled out related sentences.

I disagree with those kinds of accusations. My teacher could make more than ten readings a day. He gave out exactly the same predictions for the same person no matter how many times he did it and how many years after he did it. Even a young man could not memorize over ten thousand sentences and use them to predict things that way. My teacher worked perfectly in his seventies. He dealt with so many people every day, and the work was so strict that it allowed no exceptions. How could he work and rely upon his memories?

Once, a famous writer visited my teacher. He knew his exact minute of birth because he already had a reading from *Tie Ban Shen Suan* from somewhere. That means at the minute he was born my teacher must pull out a related sentence that fits his case. He jumped up from his chair when a sentence said that he had three mothers. He told us that in Hong Kong, almost no one knew that he had three mothers, including his girlfriend. The sentence was related to the birth minute he claimed.

Sometimes the first sentence had already matched our client's case, and my teacher had no chance to get information at all, yet predictions he pulled out were accurate. For example, a lady had her first sentence saying, "Your *father had already died before you were born*," and it matched her case. Basing on that birth time, the second sentence said, "*Your father should die from unnatural causes*." As a landlord, her father was executed by the Chinese Communist Party in 1949.

My cousin was born at home and my aunt knew exactly the minute she was born. The sentence at the related minute said that "two sisters are just like two lovely flowers." My aunt had two daughters. They were polite and lovely. They were both school teachers and had successful husbands.

My teacher always told people that he was only an operator who knew how to use a formula to pull out predictions that were written by Shao Kang Jie nine hundred years ago. It is no doubt that Shao's predictions were not made by chances. His scientific basis is much greater than we could imagine.

Shao Kang Jie's
Background and Theory

Shao Kang Jie's Background

Shao Kang Jie was born in 1011 and died in 1077. He moved around in his early life and finally settled down in the capital, Luo Yang (洛阳). When he was young, he already knew that he was a genius who would have important achievements. Shao read all the books he could find. He forced himself to live in a tough environment to strengthen his will. For instance, he would not set fires in the winter and refused to use fans in the summer. He hardly lay down to sleep and sat for meditation most of the time. He obtained his knowledge from books and from life as well. He traveled month by month in poor situations to visit great scholars' hometowns from all over the country.

At the time he settled in Luo Yang city, his financial situation was very bad. In order to support his parents, he earned money by selling grass or tree branches he picked up on the mountain. As a genius he suffered from hunger but never became an angry genius. He named his home *a comfortable snug* and did meditation there every day and only took a walk outside when the weather was good.

He was friendly to everybody. People knew he was coming when they heard the noise created by his wagon's wheels. Children called him "our mister," and adults prepared food for him. After his middle age, his predictions were well-known all over the country. It seemed he knew that this society will lose track of his formula eventually. He spent most of his time teaching, and nineteen of his students were successful and well-known in the Chinese history. The prime minister then built a house for him, and they always had parties there. A few times he rejected positions that the emperor offered to him. He believed those positions would give him no benefit only headaches. He preferred living in a relaxed way freely.

Shao Kang Jie's Teacher

Shao's first teacher was the governor of his hometown, Lee Ting Zi. Lee was the student of Chan Bor (陈博), a famous scholar in Chinese history. Shao made important improvements when he used I-Ching hexagrams to predict events. He gave up the popular way people used then and connected hexagrams with the eight directions in the traditional way. Besides that, an amazing experience gave him a chance to learn more.

According to the historical records, one day Shao was awakened by a rat, and he used his pillow to hit that rat. The pillow, made of china, broke, and a note fell out. The note said, "*This pillow was broken by a man named Shao Kang Jie when he was using it to hit a rat.*" The note was obviously written by someone previously. Shao was astonished by such an amazing prediction. He visited the store where he bought the pillow and located its previous owner. The previous owner had just passed away. Before he died, he told his family members to give a book to someone named Kang Jie and Shao Kang Jie would let them know where to get the money for his funeral. That was a book about I-Ching hexagrams, and only Shao knew how to read it. According to the instructions, Shao found the place where the person kept his savings.

After reading the book, Shao's theory was improved substantially. We had no way to confirm the above record. However, if we see things that Shao recorded in his book, we should not doubt about the prediction of *someone hitting a rat and breaking a pillow on a certain day.* Below is more information about Shao Kang Jie and his predictions.

Shao Kang Jie's Works and His Theory

The most important book Shao Kang Jie wrote was *Wang Chi Ching Shi Shu* (皇极经世书). A famous British scholar, Joseph Needham, introduced Shao Kang Jie in his book *Science and Civilization in China*.

In volume 2, page 595, he said, "That is a book of the sublime principle which governs all things within the world." Many years after, a Western scientist, Gottfried Wilhelm von Leibniz, the founder of the binary theory of computers, obtained Shao's book from a Western priest who had a trip to China.

The most important achievement Shao made is setting up a calendar. Shao had his particular numbers attached with each year in the calendar he set up. He believed that our universe was running in circles, and he used the word *Yuan* (元) to name it. Each *Yuan* had twelve different units named Huei (会). Each *Huei* had thirty units named *Yun* (运). In each *Yun* there were twelve *Shi* (世) and every *Shi* had thirty years. Altogether, one circle contained 120,600 years. In this way, not even one day in his calendar system was the same because it will belong to either a different month, a different year, a different *Shi*, a different *Yun*, a different *Huei*, or a different *Yuan*. He then used numbers to identify every single day in his huge calendar system.

It is said he could compose 559,872,000 different life situations by using his system. According to his theories, during the circle of *Yuan*, things originate, grow, mature, and end. When 120,600 years were over, a circle (*Yuan*) is ended. After that a new circle will start. For Shao, our universe has no beginning and ending time but runs in circles. He believed that today's human society is in about the seventy thousand year of our circle.

Shao Kang Jie's book *Wang Chi Ching Shi Shu* included twelve volumes. In the first to the sixth volumes he approved that all the important historical events matched the outcome of his predictions from calculations. He then made predictions for the future events such as what I introduced previously in this book. As I knew most of his predictions came out true. Unquestionably he had successfully proved that life events are predestined, such as writing down that person who was born at my birth minute has a husband twelve years younger than me.

In the seventh to ninth volumes, he categorized all the physical things—animals, birds, plants, worms, voices, and rocks—into different hexagrams. He also categorized different noises and used them to set up hexagrams. What I mentioned before, that the death of a king could be predicted based on the ringing of a bell, was based on a similar theory.

In the eleventh and twelfth volumes, Shao stated his philo-sophical, political, and historical opinions and explained the origination of our universe. It contained some important physics and math knowledge.

For Shao, all hexagrams link with certain numbers composed from an individual's birth time or the thing's forming time. As what we said previously since, every five-minute time trait is a different fate of an individual, and things are different. Shao's system was commanded by his students as knowledge. People after him continued to add new predictions in *Tie Ban Shen Suan* and created different editions. Again, those predictions were proven correct in the past nine hundred years.

Unfortunately, there are less than ten Chinese who know how to use Shao's formula today and none of them know how Shao's theory worked. We do not know how compose numbers for the related omens. We do not know how to set up hexagrams and how to predict life's events by interpreting hexagrams. Most people even refuse to believe the system works. They do not recognize Shao's achievement because they don't believe and could not explain why events are predestined.

Events Predicted by Shao Kang Jie

Shao Kang Jie not only could predicted people's lives based on their birth time, he could predict all events using related omens and hexagrams. He picked up omens we encountered and set up hexagrams based on the factors of that an unusual event, such as its happening time, direction, and subject. Those hexagrams helped him make the predictions. Below are records about him.

One day, two birds fell onto the ground when they were fighting each other. Birds can fly, and it was unusual that they fell to the ground. Shao used the day and the time that the event occurred to set up a hexagram. He predicted that in that garden a girl will pick flowers at dusk the next day and break her left hip. The next day something happened exactly like what he said.

Shao saw a branch fall from a big tree with no wind. He set up a hexagram based on the object (a tree), the direction (west), and the time of the event. He predicted that within ten days that tree would be cut down. Exactly on the tenth day of building a temple there, people cut down that tree.

One midnight, Shao heard a cow moo sadly from the north. He set up a hexagram predicting that the cow would be killed within twenty-one days. On the twentieth day someone bought the cow and killed it. The same prediction about a cock was also correct.

Once, Shao and his friends stood in front of some blooming flowers. His friend asked him, "Do these beautiful flowers also have a predestined fate?" Shao set up hexagrams based on the time when his friend asked the question and based on the numbers of the words his friend used in his sentence. He predicted that on the next day at noon those flowers would be destroyed by horses. The owner of the garden was upset and reminded all his guests to tie up their horses well. At lunch time of the next day, the owner's horse jumped out of its stable and stepped on those flowers.

Another time, Shao saw a character in a sign of a temple miss a draw. Based on the number of the draws in the sign he set up a hexagram. He concluded that a spirit haunted that temple. According to Shao's instruction people in the temple put the missed draw back in their sign and sent the spirit away.

Shao once figured out that at lunch time of the next day, one of his cups would be broken. He wanted to see if he could change such a destiny. He put the cup in the middle of a table and prohibited people from approaching it. That way no one could break the cup accidentally. When lunch time came, Shao's wife was angry about Shao doing nothing but watching the cup like an idiot. She grabbed the cup and broke it before Shao realized it. She did not know that Shao was making a test.

An old man came from the southeast who had an anxious expression. Shao asked if something bad happened, and the old man said no. Shao set up a hexagram based on the subject (the old man), the direction he came from, and the time he showed up. He predicted that the man would be harmed by fish. Three days later that man died at a party due to a fish bone stuck in his throat.

Shao had another prediction about a young man who looked happy for no obvious reason. From a hexagram Shao predicted that the young man would receive a lot of money from an engagement, and that came true a few days later.

The Basic Theory of Setting Up Hexagrams

People might say that the above prediction had nothing to do with knowledge but was related to common sense. When he saw someone upset, he concluded that something bad would happen, and when he saw someone happy, he believed that the person would have good luck. Such comments are correct in some ways. Research reveals that people usually have subconscious senses for their future even though they don't know exactly what will happen. For example, people who died in accidents might look miserable a half year before things happened.

In the above cases, the old man showed unusual anxiety and the young man seemed unusually delighted. It was possible that they might not realize what would happen in the future but their subconscious could already feel that. It is because neurotransmitters that are related to the activities of subconscious could travel faster than light and reach the future ahead.

Based on omens, Shao set up and interpreted related hexagrams and then figured events that would happen in the future. What he could do, creating a connection between a man's death and fish, was far beyond what common sense could tell.

As a matter of fact, when setting up hexagrams, Shao followed strict rules. He used the traditional way to create links between the hexagrams and the directions that related to events. That was an important improvement at Shao's age. He categorized different people such as old men, young men, old women, and young women into different hexagrams. Based on his theory, everything in our world is linked to different hexagrams and every hexagram is related to a specific number. Below is the procedure for setting up hexagrams.

First, he picked up the time, direction, and related subject of the omens to set up hexagrams. Using the numbers that relate to the hexagrams, he composed a sum and then divided the sum by six. If there was remainder, that meant a certain diagram in the hexagram was supposed to switch between yin and yang. Then we can interpret hexagrams and obtain specific information about future events.

It is difficult to explain his theory and method in a few paragraphs. Actually, I just know how to compose the hexagrams, and I don't know how to interpret them. I give a short introduction here to explain that we have to follow rules when setting up hexagrams. Presages did have some meaning in our life. How to predict the future through them is a new topic for us.

After September 11, 2001, an architect sent a letter to a Chinese newspaper, *World Journal*, in New York, which reported his experience when his team displayed the demo of the World Trade Center to the public. In front of him a child put a paper airplane on the demo and said, "Bomb." That unusual behavior caught his attention and made him feel very uncomfortable. When the World Trade Center was destroyed by airplanes on 9/11, he recalled the child's behavior and felt horrified. He couldn't help but disclose what he saw, and I considered that an omen.

According to Shao's theory, the finishing time of a building would determine its fate. The entities in the subatomic world have already seen what would happen to the World Trade Center. They conveyed that message through a child who had weak consciousness. Usually an adult's consciousness would be strong enough to reject messages from the spirit world. They would not act weirdly and put a paper airplane on the demo of the World Trade Center.

Believing that the World Trade Center was destined to collapse does not mean that I forgive what the terrorists did. I just wonder why the FBI ignored warnings regarding of that again and again. Why they could successfully stop terrorists' plots previously but not this time. Presages are messages conveyed by spirits from the other world. It is hard to change the predestined event.

Events that happen on earth are shown all at once in the world beyond the atom. That is why entities from the other world were able to record historical events three thousand years ago when they wrote the Bible. Spirits can travel in the time dimension; they thus are able to preview events. One of my friends claimed that before 9/11, two deceased people conveyed the message to her in a dream. Her best friend handed her a videotape that showed the scenario of 9/11. Her mother also told her that a big fire would happen near her neighborhood. It is no doubt that spirits exist somewhere and they can preview events on earth over there. They might communicate with us by creating omens or contacting us in dreams.

It is said that adding up the year, month, and day together, the disasters that happened in China in 2008—snow, earthquake, and riots in Tibet—all had the final number nine. For example, the date of the earthquake, May 12, 2008, added up was 9 (5+12+2+8=18 and 1+8=9) as well as April 13, 2008. Numerology considers nine an extreme figure that means important things might happen. I put data here to prove that using I-Ching to set up hexagrams based on figures and omens has its absolute reasons. I-Ching theory is too complicated and too great to be invented by the human brain. I believed that was a gift from the world beyond the atom.

In Chinese history, Weng King (文王) is the first person to interpret hexagrams. He prayed and finished the job when he was in jail. I-Ching was considered knowledge and respected by most scholars in ancient China. It was even recommended by emperors in many dynasties. I-Ching was used to make predictions. I am proud that my great-grandfather Qi Yuan Chan (陈启源) was familiar with that. He had a book (理气索源) that discussed the theory related to chi and physical things.

The Chinese also deal with occult force when they need help. Monks and Taoist priests are mediums who created the connections. Unfortunately dealing with occult forces are bent by the government because it contradicts materialism that the Communist party recommends. They do not like people to know the truth as well as our scientists.

Psychic and Occult Reports
in Ancient China

There are many psychic phenomena that were recorded in ancient China. People's psychic's ability was much more powerful and popular than today. Besides getting abilities from training, they got help from the occult force.

People could see performance in the street such as psychics sliding on small matchboxes that were made of a carton. They moved so fast that people could not even see their faces clearly. Those matchboxes were not crushed after being stepped on. It looked like the performers had overcome gravity and floated on the matchboxes rather than stepped on them. They could also step on the flames of candles as well. Psychics could make plants grow in a second. They could make a plant bloom and grow with some cucumbers and not far from them where they grew some cucumbers. Psychics could even cut someone to pieces and reconnect them later.

According to a report in a famous Chinese history book, in the Song period, a person named Du Si Sheng usually gave a demonstration after his audience purchased a certain number of mules from him. His performance included cutting off his son's head and reconnecting it to his mules. Once, after cutting off his son's head and putting it on a mule, his son did not jump up as he usually did. Du Si Sheng told his audience to stop playing games with him. His son still did not wake up. Du Si Sheng grabbed some soil and made a gourd grow up from the soil promptly. He then made another plea, and the child was still lying on the ground. Du said, "I have no other choice but beg your pardon." He cut the gourd, and at the same time, among his audience, a monk's head fell to the ground; after that Du's son came back to life.

This data sounds unbelievable. However, it was similar to a demonstration I saw on the internet. Mr. David Blaine could take a chicken's head off and put it back. The chicken was still alive after all those things were done. He could take his heart out from his chest, and he could take his audience's teeth off and put them back. Everything was caught by the camera intensively.

These kinds of demonstrations could be seen on the street easily in ancient China. Most of them relate to Taoism. A famous psychic, Ge Hong (葛洪), listed all the magic ability in his book *Bao Bu Zi*. It said that the psychics could float in the air and fly, could be in different places at the same time, and could become invisible as well as make objects invisible. They could change people's sex just by smiling. Their frowning could make them change to an old person, and their crouching could make them change to a baby. They could also be change to birds, animals, trees, rocks, etc. They could turn a cane into wood. They could make vegetables grow and ripen in a minute.

Joseph Needham, a famous English scholar, also quoted a similar report in his book *Science and Civilization in China* (section 10, I). It said:

> Liu An, Prince of Huainan, liked see to see psychics' performance. They could make a river flow simply by drawing a line on the ground; could gather up earth to form mountains and precipices; could use their breathing to influence the temperature, inducing winter or summer at will; could create rain of fog by making sneeze or and coughing. Most of those psychics were Taoist.

Taoism's founder was Lao Zhi (老子). It is said when Lao Zhi's mother was pregnant, she saw plenty of meteorites, and one of the meteorites dropped into her mouth. Lao Zhi was much taller than regular people. He could keep his servant alive for two hundred years. Once, his servant asked for a large sum of money from him. Lao pointed his finger at his servant, and his servant turned into a skeleton immediately.

Taoists believe that all physical beings are made of chi. In the range of the gravity field, things exist as physical beings. However, beyond the gravity field, things exist as chi. Taoists practice how to pass in and out of the gravity field. They could apport and asport things or change the physical look of things by *playing with chi*.

The psychics might get help from spirits when dealing with things on the chi (yin) level because spirits are in the yin world. In ancient China, the famous psychics had to perform in front of emperors, and their abilities were recorded by the palace. If they used trickery, they were killed.

In the San Kuo (三国) period, a magician named Zhuo Qi provided a demonstration to his emperor, Chao. Right before lunch time, Chao said that he needed Lu fish. Lu fish only lived in the Shong River, which was a few thousand miles away from Chao's palace. Zhuo Qi asked for a pot of water and pretended that he was fishing. After a while, a live Lu fish appeared on his fishing rod. The king asked for more fish. Zhuo Qi changed his bait and caught more. Chao then asked for ginjing, a product from a hundred miles away. Zhuo was able to present that kind of ginjing to Chao immediately.

Another time Chao and Zhuo Qi went to a barbecue together. Zhuo entertained Chao's security guards with a bottle of wine and a piece of meat. When all those people were full and drunk, Zhuo still had wine and meat in his hand. Later the king found that the food he prepared for himself was all gone. It was obvious that the meat and wine Zhou used to entertain people belonged to Chao. Chao was embarrassed and angry. He ordered his guards to kill Zhou. Zhou hit his head against the wall and disappeared. Chao hunted Zhou, and Zhou turned himself into an old man. Chao gave orders to kill the old man. Zhou made everybody in the street look like the same old man.

In the Tang period, a person named Hang Xiang also had magical powers. Before Hang Xiang was born, a psychic had already said that Hang's family would have one famous poet and one famous fairy (in ancient China they called people who had psychic ability fairies).

The wine in Hang Xiang's wine bottle was never empty no matter how many people drank from it. He could make flowers grow in a fire pot. It is said that when he was born his mother saw a few people who were surrounded by light. Since Hang Yu was a famous historical person, the Chinese people also considered Hang Xiang and his psychic ability as authentic.

Another famous psychic, Yie Fa Shang, was born in the Tang period. He once died for five days when he was seven years old. His father and grandfather were both Taoists. However, his outstanding psychic ability came from a man who was surrounded by some special light.

In the Nanch'ao period (Southern Dynasties), psychic Lu Fa He's dead body disappeared from his coffin that had been buried. Lu Fa was also a prophet. He predicted that in his period, three kings would come from the same mother and rule the country by turns. Two of them served on the throne for only five years altogether. Things happened exactly like he predicted.

Another psychic refused to entertain his king with his magic ability. The king sent someone to summon him. The physic made himself die in front of those people. The king's messengers wouldn't leave until the psychic's body decomposed. However, after a few days, people saw that psychic walk in the street again.

Once, in a specific festival, Yie Fa Shang followed his king to see a light fair in the streets. He told the king that the street fair was much more beautiful in Gang Su province. He could take the king there if the king closed his eyes. They traveled a few hundred miles in a second and reached Gang Su. In a restaurant of Gang Su, the king used his personal item in exchange for some wine because he did not have cash with him.

The next day the king doubted that Yie Fa Shang simply created an illusion on him. To verify the experience in the previous night, he sent someone to investigate in Gang Shu. In the restaurant they really found the king's personal item. This record was kept officially and was recognized by the king. It disclosed that humans could travel promptly disregarding distance.

These reports from ancient times could not be verified and thus sounded unbelievable. It is interesting that similar experiences were also recorded in the Western world. That encourages me to announce what I believe.

Chi Gong and Occult Force Reported in Modern China

After 1949, methods that the ancient Chinese used to deal with the occult force are banned by the Communist government. However, from 1980 to 1990, the Chinese government once allowed reports related to the supernatural published in the newspaper. The Central government had a leader group to control the Chi Gong Research in China. It started from a newspaper report in China.

In 1979, a newspaper in Sichuan province reported that a child, Tang Yu, could recognize Chinese characters without glancing at them but by hearing them. As more children read the news, more and more of them claimed that they had a similar ability. It is said that practicing chi gong could maintain and strengthen those kinds of abilities. In those days different reports about chi gong and supernormal events created a lot of enthusiasm in China. Some important Chinese government leaders such as Yie Jian Ying and Hu Yao Bang personally tested those chi gong and psychic abilities. Facing facts, they concluded that chi gong, as part of Chinese culture, deserved to be researched.

From 1979 to 1989, the Chinese government set up a group with four people to control the chi gong research in China. They created communication between the government and chi gong experts. They invited the well-known chi gong masters and psychics to do research. Through a lot of demonstrations, the group recognized the phenomena of healing, telekinesis, taking pills out of a sealed bottle, clairvoyance, and setting up a fire on a bare hand without any fire resources. They even let the psychics remotely explore mines in maps. It is said some of them had the accuracy of 80 percent.

Some Chinese scientists were also involved with the research. Qian Xue Sheng (钱学森), the most important nuclear physicist in China, was educated in the United States and once worked at the Massachusetts Institute of Technology (MIT) as a professor during the Second World War.

Qian sent his assistant to observe the ability of a famous psychic named Zhang Bao Sheng. For a few days and nights his assistant stayed with Zhang. He confirmed that when Zhang was in a state of sleep, he could obtain objects, such as an apple, just by grabbing the air. Qian Xue Sheng believed that some unknown energy exists inside humans' bodies. He expected researching about this energy could help our traditional scientists reach a new level. Theory related to the human body should be as important as relativity and quantum mechanics.

During those days the Chinese scientists have successfully measured rays that were emitted by chi gong masters. They also proved that those rays could kill viruses or make plants grow faster. In the medical field, different radiation rays created by equipment have been used for therapy purposes. Why can't we recognize that chi—a ray that is projected by an organic machine, like humans' physical bodies—also has a healing function? When practicing chi gong, practitioners guide chi in and out of their disease sites. As energy, chi can kill viruses, eliminate infection, and clear channel blockages in our bodies. The whole process results in healing.

Besides researching healing effects, they also noticed that there were some supernatural events that the current scientific laws could not explain. To meet scientific standards, the researchers repeated the tests and recorded the results carefully. For example, in order to find out how pills were removed from a sealed bottle, they used a high-speed camera that can take four hundred pictures within a second. That way they could see when a pill was leaving the bottle at about three millimeters away. Out of fifty tests they successful caught the moment seven times.

In order to research psychics' telemetric ability, they triple folded more than a hundred pieces of paper with Chinese characters printed on them and put them in an envelope. They pulled things out randomly with a machine and made sure no one knew what the word is. The test showed four people could tell what the character was in the triple-folded paper. One person got 60 percent correct and the best one got 95 percent correct. Working a long time could make the psychics exhausted and fail the tests. Their telemetric ability might be strong on one day but weak on another.

People in the scientific group believed that chi was some unknown energy that has a major relationship with biological beings such as the human body. They also agree that chi gong exercise could enhance psychic ability.

Qian Xie Sheng (钱学森) believed that *human bodies are not only made up of the three basic molecules, they also contain energy like biological magnetic rays.*

They explain chi gong internal excise in a scientific way:

Basically, blood circulating throughout our body for one complete circulation needs about 250 cubic centimeters of oxygen. The amount of oxygen it requires is more than what our regular breathing is able to provide. The benefit of physical exercise is to force us to inhale more oxygen. However, physical exercises meanwhile exhaust our energy, and deep respiration doesn't. In other words, chi gong internal exercise encourages deep breathing that helps us obtain a large amount of oxygen and costs almost no energy. Chinese people believe that air contains nutrition that can nourish our chi, which is an important element of our body.

During those days, a lot of reports related to chi gong were published in China because of Qian's encouragement. Data I provide here relates to experiments monitored by Chinese officers who are loyal to their government. They have no reason to tell lies for confirming a theory that their government does not like.

Reports below were published in newspapers during those days. They included abstaining from food, apporting objects, and psychic healing.

Reports about Abstaining Food

In 1981 after attending a chi gong seminar, a thirteen-year-old Chinese girl, Xiao Ding (小丁), did not expect to obtain any chi gong ability, yet she vomited as long as she ate. It is amazing that without food she felt she had more energy. The situation lasted for almost two years.

A government's chi gong group assigned twenty people, included a medical doctor from the United States, to observe Xiao Ding's daily schedule intensively. They followed her twenty-four hours a day. Every two minutes they made tests involved with twenty-eight kinds of basic nutrition that human body consisted. More than a hundred kinds of tests were conducted on Xiao Ding as well as on a control group. For using some better equipment, they took tests in other cities beside Beijing.

They confirmed that Ding just had 5 percent of the recommended daily nutritional allowance. She was able to run her regular schedule because her metabolism was slowed down and was even negative sometimes.

Another government officer, Zhang Jian (张剑), also rejected food after practicing chi gong.

Zhang once was so sick that no drugs or herbs can heal him. The more medicine he took, the higher index shown in his tests. He could hardly walk and had to stay in bed most of the time. He total recovered after he started to practice chi gong in 1982. As a professor he carefully recorded his experiences, including abstain-ing from food.

In December 1987, Zhang Jian vomited when in front of food. As a result, he ate nothing for eighteen days. The university he worked for set up a medical group to take care of him during emergencies. They measured his blood pressure every two days. Zhang Jiang believed that in those days he actually absorbed universal energy through his skin pores. Every day between four and eight in the afternoon some kind of energy went in and out of his body. Besides breathing with his mouth or nose, he could also absorb oxygen through his skin pores that made him feel warm and comfortable. People in his room could also feel the warmth.

Many years after, I personally met a disciple in a temple, she did not eat for a year as well, and she told me she maintained her daily routine perfectly. We both believe her yin body and her skin pores observed nutrition she needed from the air and made her yang body working well.

In ancient China, when Taoists got psychic training, they had to abstaining from food. It could make practitioners run faster or enhance their senses. In modern China, some people healed their long-term illness by abstaining from food for a certain period. Some theory holds that abstaining from food can help people overcome different kinds of illnesses, such as high blood pressure and stomach infection.

Abstaining from food can reduce the pressures caused by digestion. Digestion exhausted energy. Extra food left in our body actually creates many problems. Zhang Jian's case proved that energy could be absorbed from the universe subconsciously. Abstaining from food for a short period of time thus would not harm but improve our health.

Reported Relation to Psychic Ability

After practicing chi gong, Zhang Jian was more sensitive, and it seemed he had psychic abilities.

For example, he could see a tumor, existing like some black energy, in the right side of his coworker's body. However his coworker claimed that the pain was from the left side. Later, a medical report proved that his coworker's right intestinal canal had cancer, and his left side was fine. Such kind of experience happened for several times.

During those days, he lost sense about space as well. When he physically sat in one place, he felt that he was somewhere else simultaneously. The division between his physical body and the outside world was not clear, and he thus was very sensitive to the environment around him. For example, when a sick child got into his room, his left arm became very cold. The blood pressure in his two arms was obviously different. One was 80/120 and the other was 140/180. That child had a high fever and required a treatment from him. He believed that his left arm had absorbed the sick energy from the child. It was amazing that soon after leaving Zhang Jian's home, the child's temperature went down.

He also had clairvoyance. Sitting at home, Zhang could tell where his son was in his honeymoon, such as when they were supposed to go home, they returned to Yellow Mountain all of a sudden. His son was surprised about what Zhang Jian said because they themselves even did not know where to go until the last moment.

Zhang Jian had another interesting and important experience. His supervisor did not believe in chi gong but asked for a psychic reading. Zhang Jian could not see through the supervisor's physical body like he usually did with others. Instead, Zhang felt that energy he sent out was bounced back, and that gave him a headache. They had to give up the test and talked about something else. When they were not intent to do the test, Zhang Jian's energy was not blocked, and he easily found out the supervisor's health problems. During a relaxing conversation, the supervisor was not in a defensive state and didn't project energy to resist Zhang's energy. This story proved that chi could reject each other. That is why some chi gong experts failed their demonstrations in front of those hostile to him. That also explains why it requires faith when people requested help from chi gong experts.

Another famous psychic in modern China, Zhang Bao Sheng, could apport things by intense desiring. He could give his audience a hundred pounds of sugar without even getting up from his chair. The bag of sugar was stored in the next room. No one in the audience saw him go out of the room, and no one saw a bag was delivered to him in the demonstration.

He passed through a wall in front of forty college students. Those students watched all the entrances intensely to prevent him from getting into an auditorium through a door. He disappeared all of a sudden when he was talking to the people around him. Almost at the same time, he appeared on the other side of the wall inside the auditorium. People later found that there was a print of someone's body on the wall.

Zhang's ability makes me think of a new phenomenon in physics tunneling. During that moment a particle disappears in front of its barrier and reappears on the other side immediately. Zhang could take pills out of a sealed bottle. Money automatically moved to Zhang's pocket when he passed by a bank teller's window. When he was young, he was poor but hoped he could buy a pair of shoes for his girlfriend. As a result, that pair of shoes was placed in his handbag. He lost his policeman job because of that "stealing." Since then Zhang realized that if he wished to have something, those things would come automatically. He did not know how, and since then he had psychic ability. He only knew that when his mother was pregnant with him, some blue light was approaching her.

Hou Jing Guei was one of the greatest psychics in modern China. He was able to make bills float into the auditorium from an open window. Those bills were issued by fourteen different coun-tries. He had to return those bills by making them disappear in a second.

Hou Jing Guei could obtain whatever his audiences requested in the show, such as cigarettes produced from a remote province in China. He apported famous dishes and wine that were only existed in ancient China. Audiences usually request things that could not be found in the local market, and they did not tell what they need before the demonstration. Yet Hou could apport things in a second. According to the report people in the demonstration were smart news reporters or successful businessmen in Hong Kong. They all accepted that Hou had his psychic ability and was not cheating.

Hou Jing Guei was from a family that performed psychic street shows before 1950. He was a performer when he was a child. We have not heard from Hou for many years. An official article once disclosed that Ho Jing Guei was in jail because he stole guns. I saw another person who claimed that in jail he met someone who could get a roast duck by grabbing the air.

Reports about Healing

Chi gong ability that had psychic power could be obtained by training. One of the famous healers in China, Lu Xing Lin, was from a traditional medical family. His father and two uncles both practiced healing. Lu was trained strictly since he was five years old. Every day, he had to hit, push, and draw green beans in a big pot to enhance the energy in his palms. When the skin of the green beans all came off, he refilled the pot with some sand and repeated the same practices. The practice made his nails turn from red to purple and then dark. The dark nails fell off and new nails grew. Besides hitting beans and sand, he also hit walls, trees, and rocks. The energy he used for healing was accumulated from these kinds of exercises.

He was a professional swimming teacher and a healer as well. In order to maximize the healing result, he sent his chi to some particular acupuncture points. He even used his energy to destroy cancer cells. One of his patients was a teacher, Wang Mei Lian, who had cancer cells still spread to her left lung, causing fluid retention and giving her swelling and pain. After being treated by Mr. Lu for thirty times, she could eat and sleep well. Her pain was gone, and the fluid retained in her lung disappeared. The two scars in her lung were no longer found in the x-ray pictures.

From October 1987 to January 1988, there were 347 cancer patients who had been treated by Lu Xing Lin. Most of them were considered hopeless by Western medicine but were obviously improved under Lu's healing. Some of them 100 percent recovered.

Photos showed that during the treatment Lu had to accumulate all his energy in his palms and project it to his patients' malignancies. He was shouting loudly, and it seemed that he was pushing the bad cancer energy out of the disease sites. He only spent one minute on each patient, yet the healing result was obvious. Mr. Lu also used the same principle to treat diabetes—pulled out the sick energy and sent the healthy energy to his patients' kidneys. Results for that were also amazing.

Chinese medical theories believe that disease is caused by bad energy. Lu's basic theory was to remove sick energy from patients' bodies. His healing power was obtained from long-term exercises. His healing methods had nothing to do with the occult force and solely depended on Chinese acupuncture or medical theory.

In ancient China, many people got psychic power through tough trainings. They had strong motivation and environments that were without distractions. The Chinese hardly have such moti-vation today. No one likes to obtain healing ability though tough training and being attacked by the supernatural later. Chinese Taoists did have some methods to enforce people's psychic abilities that had something to do with occult force. They lost track in China today just like the fate that *Tie Ban Shen Suan* has. It is regrettable to see a great culture is abandoned like that.

Healers and the Occult Force

However, still some healers referred their psychic ability to occult forces such as spirits and angels from the world beyond the atom. The Chinese government could not accept such opinions under any circumstances. At around 1980, there was a famous psychic healer, Zhang Xiang Yu (张香玉), who used her psychic ability to heal hundreds of patients, and she was arrested by the government eventually.

In 1978, ⊠ started to practice chi gong internal exercises. She prayed to the sky in a park one day and asked if her life would be finished at her forties. All of a sudden, some amazing things happened: Zhang pirouetted very fast on her toes and made some weird postures meanwhile. She could not stop herself and was considered crazy by people around her.

Since that day, her hands released some kind of blue ray that could be confirmed by the other people as well. When she held the straphanger handle on the bus, other passengers felt electricity and would take their hands away immediately. When she touched the heat radiator at home, everybody in that house felt some hot unknown energy. Those energies gave her the ability to heal illnesses that medicine could not heal.

A young man, Lee Xing Zhong, had a serious kidney infection. He could not even stand up the first time he visited Zhang. Zhang saw some black energy was in Lee's kidney as well as her students. When Zhang processed the healing, black energy was released from Lee's body. After visiting Zhang two times Lee could practice chi gong exercises. He was totally recovered after receiving eight treatments. The patient Lee introduced his experience to correspondents and hoped to publish those experiences.

One of Zhang's students, Lee Li Hong, was a former professional athlete who collapsed due to overexercising. She passed out constantly, and her heartbeat was irregular. Different tests showed that her health condition was very bad. During the healing, Zhang drew three circles in front of Lee Hong's face and said some language that no one ever heard. Lee felt some warm energy flow into her body, and she totally recovered within two weeks. Since then Lee Ho had healing power as well.

Lee's husband had a retinal infection. Zhang Xiang Yu grabbed the air in front of him as if she was pulling things out of his eyes. After she did that a few times, Lee's husband could see well and since then he had healing ability to heal broken bones by just touching his patients.

Zhang claimed that her healing ability simply came from a guiding spirit. It had nothing to do with chi gong exercise. Her healing power can be transferred to people who never practice chi gong. However, in order to gain the healing power, her students must have strong faith in her. For that reason, she was attacked by the authorities. Below are the conversations between Zhang Xiang Yu and the people who convicted her.

Interrogator:	Who is your guiding spirit?
Zhang:	Someone who passed away years ago.
Interrogator:	Can those people talk to you now?
Zhang:	No, they cannot. Even children know that.
Interrogator:	Then, how can they communicate with you?
Zhang:	I have no idea.
Interrogator:	What is the language you used for "healing"? You told people that is a universal language.
Zhang:	That is correct. I also used it to communicate with flowers and trees.
Interrogator:	What kind of language did you use to express yourself when you communicate with flowers and trees?
Zhang:	Chinese.
Interrogator:	So, do you think you could use your language to communicate with the flowers and trees in the United States?

Zhang was silent when being asked that kind of question. She finally admitted that she was a crook and stopped her practice related to healing.

My arguments related to this case are listed as below.

1. Zhang did carry energy that the other people could detect.
2. The energy Zhang carried can heal illnesses and might be able to be conveyed to her patients.
3. The fee Zhang charged was much cheaper than what the hospital charged.

Still they got trouble. Instead of researching the blue ray that Zhang carried, the Chinese government put Zhang in jail. That is the general ending for people who recognize the occult force in China. Zhao Xue Zhong (赵学忠) was reported by the media in those days. After practicing chi gong for only three days, he acquired the healing power. Zhao could tell where his patients were from and what their problems were before they said anything. The news correspondent who reported about Zhao was also Zhao's patient. Below was what he saw in Zhao's clinic.

A man could not help groaning when was carried into the clinic. Ten minutes later he walked away and claimed that during the treatment, he felt some cool energy move down to his feet and go out of his body.

Zhao told his story to the correspondent. Before practicing chi gong, one side of Zhao's body was paralyzed. He had heart disease, and one of his kidneys was cracked. He was so sick that even the chi gong instructors refused to accept him as a student. He must promise that if he got side effects, he would not blame it on anybody. After practicing chi gong for just a few days, some energy made him feel hot, and he felt that he could fly. He could not stop doing those chi gong routines. He moved crazily and was so powerful that seven people could not control him. He did not eat or sleep like he usually did, yet he did not feel exhausted. He could run a few hundred meters at his maximum speed easily. Soon after that, light bulbs or a TV around him could not even function. Almost at the same time he was able to tell people's illnesses without asking them any questions.

One day he saw a tumor on his coworker's stomach, and his words were proven by an x-ray result. Instead of taking the medical treatment, his coworker got healing from Zhao. His tumor disappeared after have five times treatments from Zhao.

Even Zhao himself did not believe the healing ability he had. He mentioned that to his mother who had strokes. Her mother requested healing from Zhao. After one month, she could get off the bed and take care of housework. It was amazing that for many years since then she had vigorous health.

Once Zhao saw a woman was crying on the way to a hospital. Without an inquiry, Zhao knew that the woman had heart disease but pain came from her nervous system. Zhao gave them a free treatment and told them to forget about the hospital. Even Zhao himself did not understand why he took that kind of action. He said to the news reporter, "I must be controlled by something and lost my mind then. I even told them that I was an herbalist. If the treatment I provided did not work and something happened to that woman, how could I take the responsibility? I did that not for money but for some other reasons!"

That was only one of the cases that Zhao handled in those days. Many times, Zhao provided free healing to strangers. For example, a man sold his only horse to pay medical fees for his wife. When they reached Zhao's office, the register window was closed. Their seven-year-old son cried loudly and that got Zhao's attention. Zhao provided free treatments and free medicine to the woman until she totally recovered.

Zhao Xue Zhong did that because he had the same experience when he was a kid. Zhao was very poor and sick in his childhood. His spleen was abnormal, and that caused his abdomen to swell. His mother sold all their family possessions to pay the medical fees. Noticing the family's poverty, an herbalist offered free treatments and medicine to Zhao. When Zhao mentioned that experience, he was tearing in front of the journalist who interviewed him. Zhao said that he still remembered the face of the herbalist who saved his life. That was why Zhao wanted so much to heal patients. Most of the illnesses he healed related to neuron malfunctions, such as a vegetative state, blindness, and paralysis.

Zhao's assistant Guo Guei Qing had a tumor on her spine that could kill her within a few months. An operation might save her life but would make her become paraplegic forever. Mr. Zhao's healing made her tumor disappear, and Guo got psychic ability herself amazingly. She told the correspondent that she must spend the rest of her life healing people because from the day she was supposed to die or become paralyzed and got the tumor, her life no longer belonged to her. She felt as if Zhao did not give her the treatments.

A famous Chinese medical professor did a lot of research on Zhao Xue Zhong. He confirmed that compared with other chi gong masters, Zhao's ability was outstanding. Zhao could know a patient's health problems in a few seconds. His diagnoses agreed with tests done by the hospital. The healers I mentioned above, Chang Xiang Yu, Zhao Xue Zhong, and Zhao's assistant, were all very sick once. They knew the feelings of being sick and had strong sympathy for the poor and the sick. They meant to help those people through their psychic healing ability. I believe the amazing results they achieved relate to the blue energy inside their bodies. Those powers came occasionally and could be transferred from one person to another. That means the power was not accumulated from chi gong internal exercises but came from an outside source.

People who believe in the occult forces argued this way: if chi can be accumulated in chi gong exercise, why do many chi gong practitioners not have even a bit of healing power even though they've practiced chi gong for a long time? Why after practicing chi gong for just a few days some were able to heal and their ability was obtained from somewhere all of a sudden? Their amazing experiences made them strongly believe that the chi is from the occult force in the world beyond the atom. Do those psychic or healing powers relate to something else?

Another report during that time answers our question.

Another well-known Chinese healer, Zhang Wei Xiang (张维祥), never practiced chi gong and had no medical knowledge as well. His healing had nothing to do with and was not related to medical theory like treatments Lu Sing Lin (the swimming teacher). All he did was give his patients a note. First it reminded people not to be superstitious. It then listed the illnesses he could heal and the rules his patients had to follow. He required medical records from his patients and provided three treatments in fifteen days. After that his patients would recover.

Zhang Wei Xiang gave absentee healing as well. A famous chi gong master, Lee Yong, once tested Zhang's healing ability. Lee's daughter-in-law was a supervisor of a nursing department in a hospital. She suffered from a stomach infection for eight years. Every time she ate she felt pain, and no medicine could stop it. Fifteen days after that she received Zhang Wei Xiang's rules *for healing*, and her stomach did not feel pain anymore. A woman had swelling in her ovaries. She got help from ten different hospitals, and all the doctors convinced her to remove her ovaries. She was healed by the rules for healing within fifteen days, and she got pregnant later.

A professor at a geography college, Zhu, in Beijing told the news reporter about his wife's experiences. His wife attempted suicide a few times because the pain in her nervous system was killing her. Zhu's daughter requested an absentee treatment from Zhang. Ms. Zhu felt hot when she received the note of healing. On the same night, she dreamed of an old man putting an acupuncture needle into her head. Since then her pain was gone completely.

Lee Jing Rong, a captain in a military bureau, told how Zhang Wei Xiang healed his whole family. Lee's son had a psychosis that got worse day by day. He was very perplexed, melancholic, restless, and could not sleep. The sleeping pills he took were double the limit yet they still did not work. He got fatter, tired, and did not know what he was doing. Zhang gave him the same note of healing and told him to stop taking the sleeping pills. Later his son consistently vomited some sour water for seventy hours. That kind of vomiting continued on and off for fifteen days. After that he could sleep well, lost all his excess weight, and went back to work. His health was better ever since then; he did not get sick at all for many years.

Lee's daughter-in-law had heart disease, an abnormal rhythm that made her feel tired and scared easily. Sometimes she could not even move. After receiving Zhang's note, she completely recovered. His wife who was asthmatic and had emphysema for more than twenty years was also healed by Zhang.

How did Zhang obtain his healing ability? During the Cultural Revolution in China, Zhang was assigned to work in the country where he learned to be a veterinarian. He knew only animals' acupuncture veins and arteries. He gave people treatments once in a while for emergency reasons. A game that people always played over there got Zhang's attention. In the game, four people slightly rest their fingertips on a plate that was placed upside down on a board with words. The plate could move automatically and stop in front of some words that related to questions they asked. People used that way to see their futures. Children could move the plate easier than adults and bring up decent answers even though they did not quite understand what the questions were. This game is similar to the Ouija board in the Western world.

Zhang Wei Xiang was curious about how a plate could move automatically and predict the future correctly. One night, when he thought of the same question, a plate automatically moved to him. It moved on a newspaper and stopped in front of characters that indicated answers for his questions. It said, "*There were entities higher than humanity.*" That kind of communication happened a few times. One day the plate indicated that he could receive their message by automatic writing instead of waiting for the plate to move.

Zhang asked, "How can I believe in your existence?" His hands wrote down: "We had the ability to heal."

Zhang asked, "How?"

His hands wrote down, "No medicine and no superstition. You just hand out a note that included our rules for healing. We will take care of your patients in three to seven days."

Zhang gave the note to a psychotic patient who recovered totally later. Since then Zhang started practicing healing, and he hoped to contact the entities directly. However, every time he requested it, his hand stopped writing. One day Zhang heard a female say that they would let him hear their voice. For almost two years he tried but could not locate the source of that voice. The voice was always somewhere, not too far and not too near. It spoke not too fast and not too slow. Its tone was not high and was not low. He had no problem hearing it even in noisy environments.

In 1988, the Central Government's chi gong leader group invited Zhang Wei Xiang to the capital, Beijing. They let him perform his healing ability and reported his experience in military bases. They gave him funds to do further research. The illnesses he could treat included psychosis, epilepsy, paralysis, hemiplegia, nephritis, apoplexy, renal calculus, brain atrophy, asthma, emphysema, and many other unusual illnesses. Again, if his healing ability did not work, he could not have that kind honor from the government and army during that time.

Zhang was once prosecuted by the government and was discharged later. The government could not tolerate Zhang attributing his healing power to occult forces. Since then we were unable to hear any news related to him.

Healers in the Western society have much a better practice environment. Today most religious people actually recognize psychic healing that occurred in religious meetings and consider that was power from God. My coworker Mrs. H once told me her experiences with an Indian pastor, Benny Hinn. I believe in what she said because she was a serious accountant who does not allow mistakes in her work.

Once she planned to go to Benny Hinn's meeting in Santiago. She ended up stuck in Los Angeles because she was very sick and could not eat or drink for five days. In the hotel she still tried to watch the healing meeting through a TV channel. Amazingly she heard Benny Hinn say in the meeting, "I know that a woman has been sick for five days. If she touches the TV, I can help her." She put her hands on the TV and felt energy fill her body. At the end of that day she was totally recovered. Since that day she watched every show related to Benny Hinn on the Discovery Channel and personally attended Benny Hinn's seminar as well. She told me in the meeting when Mr. Benny Hinn pushed his hands toward the people, all the people in the front fell down. Her son was right over there, and he said that he was pushed by some strong energy at that moment.

Psychic Ability Reported
in the Western World

Psychic healing sounded unbelievable, but it actually exists all over the world. In Western society, the most famous one was Edgar Cayce in the beginning of the twentieth century. Edgar hardly had any medical knowledge; however, the diagnoses he made were 85 percent correct. The therapies he prescribed included osteopathy, chemotherapy, hydrotherapy, nutrition, chiropractic treatments, massage, and home remedies.

Edgar claimed that he gained his healing ability at the age of thirteen years. One day when he was reading the Bible and praying, he saw a woman surrounded by some bright light approach him. The woman said, "Tell me what you want to do the most, and I will help you to do it."

He answered, "Most of all I would like to help others, especially the children who are sick." Since then he had the healing power. Edgar Cayce did not know what he was doing during the diagnosing. He was in his altered state and let an unknown power control him. Another famous psychic healer in Brazil, Jose Pedro Arigo, could perform surgery. He claimed that his ability related to a spirit of a departed European doctor, Dr. Fritz. Entities in the world beyond the atom obviously were involved in the healing powers that we consider supernatural.

Another famous Western psychic is from Israel, Uri Geller. In his book *My Story*, he reported his personal experience in New York. On

November 9, 1973, after 6:00 p.m., a force literally transported Geller from New York City to Ossining. Almost instantaneously he traveled about thirty miles. He felt he was sucked upward, and he had no sensation in that moment. When he opened his eyes, he was dropping into his friend's home in Ossining.[31]

Uri Geller was the son of Hungarian Jewish immigrants. His psychic ability was so powerful that when he bent metal items on TV or in a radio studio demonstration, and thousands of metals were bent in his audience's homes. The phenomena were verified by some scientists and different intermediaries. It was named the Geller Effect. Geller acquired his ability since he met a person surrounded by light in his backyard at the age of three years. He insists that his energy is related to some intelligence in the cosmos.

Another report related to how humans travel instantly disregarding distance was recorded in Raymond Buckland's work *The Spirit Book*. It is said psychics making jokes wanted to know if they can also apport persons besides apporting things. They got their answer.

Charles Williams and Frank Herne successfully apported the famous medium, Mrs. Agnes Guppy, to the séance they hold. Mrs. Guppy was wearing a dressing gown, holding a pen wet with ink and looking very startled. At the same moment she disappeared in her home that was two miles away from the séance. Her friends and servants only found a slight haze that was left near the ceiling.

In Raymond Buckland's *The Spirit Book*, it also mentioned what Australian medium Charles Bailey could do. Through his guide he could apport items such as live fish, crabs and turtles, live birds sitting on eggs in their nests, and rare antiques. This is same as what Chinese history said their psychic could do.

Another well-known Western psychic was Wolf Messing in World War II. The first time he realized he had psychic power was on a train. He could not offer to buy a ticket so he submitted a blank paper to the train conductor. All the other people saw that was a blank paper and reminded the train conductor to double check it. The train conductor still believed that it was a ticket.

Wolf made the bank teller believe that a blank paper is a check and handed in 100,000 rubles to him. He made Stalin's security guards believe he was the Soviet Union's highest commander and allow him to go directly to Stalin's office. Stalin allowed him to perform in front of thousands of Russians. Newspapers reported his performance with great details. I think he was able to change the scenario that we are supposed to see by influencing the activity of our brain. Almost a century has passed and no scientist researched Wolf's psychic ability.

Today there are still a lot of psychics who can create phenomena that could not be explained by traditional scientists. On October, 30, 2007, a TV channel invited psychics to a demons-tration. Some of them could know what the others think or make the others do something. The psychics could make their audiences write down the same numbers that they have already written on a piece of paper. One psychic made his audience draw the yin-yang symbol that was printed on his arm as a tattoo. Another psychic chose his audience randomly and made them make up a name of a place related to a murder case, the killer's name, and the weapon he used. What the audience said 100 percent matched the things he wrote down in a paper. That paper was previously put in a box and was hanging on the stage during the demonstration. This psychic must travele in the time dimension and pick this scenario ahead or he was able to influence a person's thinking.

The champion in the psychic demonstration could do these things: He gave his audiences an old newspaper and meanwhile collected one-dollar bills from each of them. He put all the bills in a big plastic box and let an audience stand inside it. All the other audience could see was what the guy did. A strong wind was introduced into the box, and we could see the bills fly in the box just like snow was in the sky. He told the guy to grasp one of those flying bills and write down its serial number. He then told his audience to open the newspaper where it published his advertisement one week ago. It recorded the same number as the number on the bill the audience caught. It looked like the psychic actually experienced the scenery ahead rather than arranged the whole thing in the show because things over there were totally out of control. He could not indicate how to grasp a bill with that number, and he could not even make sure that number was included in the bills that the audiences donated.

Even the police department admitted that sometimes they got help from psychics to locate criminals. Psychics could recognize murderers when touching related pictures. They could describe the crime scenario and the modus operandi of the murderer without requesting any information. They can sense where the victim's dead body was. Some of them claimed that subconsciously related images might show up in their brains just liked what was on TV.

Before the killer *Son of Sam* was arrested, a psychic had predicted that *Son of Sam* would be accidentally caught by highway patrolmen. She also predicted that the daughter of Randolph Hearst, Patricia Hearst, would join the gang who kidnapped her to rob a bank. She once saw the number 222 and saw a barrel that had a young boy's dead body in it. Right next to it were two words *the Mars*. Two years later on February 22, a little boy's dead body was found in a barrel. Next to the body was a rock that had the words *the Mars* on it. She obtained the image before the boy was killed. Again, it proved that the scenario of the tragedy was already there, and when her soul traveled in the time dimension, she can preview it.

I wonder how come our scientists totally ignore facts that were mentioned above when they claim that seeking the truth is their goal. Psychic phenomena are worldwide and have about the same pattern. In my opinion things or people can exist nonphysical beings, yin. At that moment, they could reject gravity and have a trip at the speed of light. When existing as nonphysical beings, they lost their physical senses or shapes. In nonphysical existence, they can interfere with peoples' thinking, can change the scenery, and can change the outcome of events. Alive in the nonphysical being, they could travel in the time dimension and preview things that have not yet happened on the earth. Their yin body could get anything from anywhere when their yang body displaces in front of us no doubt. Again, if we ignore Newton's laws and accept the concept of yin, we will be able to understand the above phenomena easily.

Prophets' Predictions
in World History

In Chinese history, there are many records about psychics' predictions. They were so respectful that even the emperors got advice from them. Their abilities either were backed up by knowledge, through training, from their psychic ability by birth, or by the spirit.

In the Jin Dynasty, a prophet, Dai Yan (戴洋), once died for five days in his childhood. After that he had amazing predicting ability. (NDErs also claim that their extrasensory perception or ESP was obtained and forced after they experienced death.) He predicted in a certain year a person named Si Ma Rong would become the emperor. When things came true, the emperor invited Dai Yang to be his consultant.

Dai Yang told the emperor who should be the general commander, when he should attack their enemy, and what kind of strategies he should use in the battles. Under Dai's instructions the emperor successfully defeated his enemies. Dai once told the emperor that he should not meet any visitor on a particular day. The emperor forgot Dai's advice and was killed by a close friend on the day that Dai Yang mentioned.

At the time the emperor *Xiao Gang* was born, Dai Yang predicted that *Xiao Gang* would have thirty years of good times. He also predicted that in the year of *the* dragon, Xiao Gang would be overthrown by his enemy who had the same birthday as Xiao. Dai Yang reminded people to be careful on August 13 of the dragon year. On that day the highest commander in that country surrendered to their enemy. They united together to overthrow the emperor, Xiao Gang. That commander was born the same day as the emperor. Dai Yang wrote things down fifty years ahead before things happened.

In the Jin Dynasty, a prophet, Guo Pu (郭朴), told a person named Geng that he would became a very important man one day. Many years later Geng became the father-in-law of the emperor because his daughter became the queen. Guo Bu also predicted that Geng's family would get down when a white dog looked like a dragon and when some gold thing grew on the graves of his parents. It was true the Geng's two sons were executed when the above two things happened many years later.

Once, an important officer asked for a psychic reading from Guo Bu and was rejected. He forced Guo Bu to do it. Guo Bu announced that the officer would not live to tomorrow, and he died at lunchtime the same day.

Another prophet in the Jin Dynasty was named Fu Tu Dung. He could predict things by hearing the ringing of bells, such as who would win the war, which emperor would be captured, and when the king would die. He predicted the new emperor's fate in his poem, and predictions were proven correct many years after he died. The poem said that when a lot of grass with thorns, *Jing* (荆), will grow under the throne, the emperor would lose his power. Some years later, the plant, *Jing*, really sprouted under the emperor's throne. A rebel with the first name Jing successfully overthrew the emperor.

The poem also said that "the big ending would show under a big column." The emperor was buried appropriately after he died. When rebels got the power, they dug the emperor's grave and threw his corpse into a river. The corpse floated to a bridge and was hooked by its column. The whole scenario was mentioned in a prediction that was recorded fifty years ago before events actually happened.

Most people would not believe that the scenario of future events could be predicted with such details. It is said in the Roman period, an astrologer predicted that King Domitian would die from some steel weapon on September 18, 96. The king was mad and asked if the astrologer knew the method of his own death. The astrologer answered that his corpse would be torn by dogs. The king meant to prove that the astrologer's prediction wrong. He ordered his servants to kill the astrologer and burn his body. At the time, a storm extinguished the fire and a group of dogs tore the corpse. Things happened exactly as what the astrologer predicted. Still, no matter how carefully the king protected himself on the day of September 18, 96, he still was killed by his trusted servant in his bedroom.

Scenarios of events are predestined, and things could be proven in the codes of the Bible. In recent years, some scholars found that important historical events and people had been mentioned by the Bible three thousand years ago. A book named the Bible Code described the details. By using some particular code, we could find information about Kennedy, Clinton, Shakespeare, the Wright brothers, Edison, Newton, and Einstein. In the same page it recorded that person's name, his birthdays, and birthplaces. The murderer's name was on the same page where it mentioned Kennedy. The Bible's predicting function is recognized by many well-known scientists but was dismissed by the religious authorities themselves.

The Bible Code proves in the dimension where God exists that things that happen on the earth appear all at one time. That is why events can record events in some way. If future events have already existed somewhere and allowed God or spirits to predict them, why couldn't humans do it? In other words, why do we ignore that humans have the same ability in some way? Why should we dismiss Shao Kang Jibe's system, using knowledge to predict the future? Scientists would not do it because even they do not know the events that happened were predestined.

Astrologers were considered crooks by most scientists since Newton's laws became dominant in the world. They ignored that even Newton believed life events were determined by the movement of the planets. He did make some predictions but could not do it by formula.

Let us review Western astrological history. The emperor Hadrian in the Roman period knew a lot about astrology. He usually wrote down his prediction about events that would happen in the new year. He even knew the exact day and time he died.

An important history book, *the Anglo-Saxon Chronicle*, records the deaths of many important people that had been accurately predicted by astrologers, such as the deaths of King Kent and King Osric and the deaths of St. Egbert and the defrocked Bishop Wilfrid.

In the middle ages, many astrologers had good educational backgrounds. Nostradamus was a doctor, and his predictions still surprise many people today. One of his predictions seemed related to what happened on September 11, 2001. In 1978, I read his prediction saying that terrorists will come from the sky. The burning at forty-five degrees made the things that happened compared to hell. When I read that prediction thirty years ago, I worried that the earth facing the end. We didn't know what Nostradamus meant until 9/11 happened. People who attacked the World Trade Center were named terrorists, and they did come from the sky. New York was located at forty-five degrees on the map. Things that happened in the World Trade Center involved fire, and people inside were in hell. It is said Nostradamus's eyes could see through things, and when he made the predictions he used a mirror or water at night. His prediction impressed many people but not traditional scientists.

The Fathers of Western medicine, Hippocrates and Galen, believed that all medical doctors supposedly also knew astrology. Paracelsus, a man who had important influence during the Renaissance, believed that *if doctors did not know how planets influenced their patients' health, they should not stay in the medical field.* Astrologer Halifax received his education at Oxford. Geoffrey Chaucer, a great novelist, also wrote a book about astrology with the title of *Treatise on the Astrolabe.*

Two important astronomers, Tycho and Kepler, also researched astrology. Tycho predicted that an eclipse would occur on October 28, 1566, and cause the king of Turkey, Suleiman, to die. Suleiman really died, right before the eclipse. Pico, an important critic of astrology, died on November 17, 1494. His death was predicted by three astrologers because Mars was threatening his life. Before Gustave Adolphe seized power, Tycho had already correctly predicted that Gustave Adolphe would be the king of Sweden one day. When Kepler predicted the future for AEW Von Wallenstein, his comments stopped in the year 1633, and Wallenstein was assassinated in that year. Kepler also predicted that in May 1618, a big conflict would cause a long war because the planets and weather tend to make people fight. On May 23, 1618, people in Prague rushed into the palace and threw two chancellors out of a window. A war that lasted for thirty years started on that day. Kepler also was the astronomer who proved that the planets revolved along an elliptical path. Today, scientists recognize him as a great astronomer but ignore the fact that he was also a great astrologer. They do not know that for Kepler, being an astrologer is much more difficult than being an astronomer.

Throughout history many Western astrologers were also great, well-educated scholars. They were intelligent and made research seriously, as what we do today. There must be some reason for them to believe in astrology. Unfortunately, the knowledge and conclusions they had from their hard work are totally disregarded by scientific authorities today.

Presages and a Lesson in My Life

Actually, many important events in our life were presaged previously. Below are my experiences:

In the morning that my son was born, a baby seat fell down from my closet coincidentally. At that moment a thought flashed through my mind that my baby might be due that day. Two hours later, when I was taking a regular checkup, the doctor confirmed what I thought. I had parturition three weeks earlier than we expected.

The day before the 2001 Chinese New Year's Eve, I broke a china bowl that had the Chinese character "long life" on it. That was my father's bowl, and it had the meaning of longevity for elderly people. I did not understand why the bowl, which belonged next door in my parents' home, was placed in my kitchen and it was broken so easily. I bought an identical bowl the next day and planned to return it to my parents without telling anybody. When I walked into my mother's apartment, she surprised me by asking, "Did you find the same bowl?" I did not know why my mother knew that bowl was broken. At that time my father was eighty-five years old, ten years older than my mother. We all expected that my mother would live longer than my father. Two days after the Chinese New Year, my mother had a stroke that took her life three weeks later. A few days before she passed away, the only china spoon that had the character of "long life" on it also cracked in my sister's hand for almost no reason. I did not believe the cracking of the bowl and spoon caused my mother's death. I believe those were omens that told us what was about to happen.

In 1997, when I opened a future commodities account, my check bounced twice. A bank teller held my check against my account for thirty days instead of three days, and as a result my funds were not available. I did not know that, and I told the company to redeposit the check again. The check bounced again. Six months later, a credit card company rejected my check twice because they could not confirm the checks that I made out to a future commodities company. That caused a future commodities company to liquidate my contracts without notifying me. They also liquidated ten of my friends' contracts that were worth a half million dollars. I lost seventy thousand dollars in one day, the biggest financial loss in my life. This occurrence was related to two bounced checks, and the omens were so obvious in the beginning when I opened my future commodities account.

A few months later my apartment was burned by fire. No matter how I tried to avoid that bad luck, things still went against me. It looked like they were predestined and was much worse than I thought. I thus restudied planets in my horoscope. My bad experience drove me to confirm some ancient Chinese astrology theory. The tuition for that was half a million dollars.

Studying carefully, I found out that it was the position of the planets that caused the disaster in that year. At the time I was born, Mars was in six degrees of Virgo, and Venus was in nine degrees. Chinese astrology holds that the trait of Mars is fire that hurts Venus, which has the trait of metal. On April 26, 1997, the day my future commodities positions were liquidated, Mars moved backward (from north to south) at sixteen degrees, Venus (in nine degrees) and Mars in my horoscopes were at six degrees of Virgo. That means two Mars were squeezing Venus at that moment. When my apartment got burned, another planet that had the trait of fire (move from north to south) was at sixteen degrees of Virgo. Again two planets had the trait of fire squeezing Venus.

According to the theory of Chinese astrology, three big reasons combined together caused my troubles in 1997:

Mars was moving backward. As a matter of fact, when it moved forward to sixteen degrees, it did not give me too much trouble. The Chinese astrology theory holds that if a planet is moving backward, it is more powerful than when it is moving forward. If the influence is negative, its damage will be serious.

If a planet was squeezed by two planets with contradicting elements from it, the situation could be even more dangerous. On April 26, 1997, my Venus (with the trait of metal) was squeezed by two planets carrying the traits of fire, Mars at my time of birth in six degrees and Mars in 1997 at sixteen degrees of Virgo.

If the planet that was squeezing has the trait same as my controller planet, the trouble was even worse.

For many times in my life Mars was in sixteen degrees of Virgo and hurt my Venus. Why did the things that happened were not as bad as 1997? It is because at the other times the degree I was located did not contain the metal element, except March 24, 1997. For two times in that year, when planets carrying the fire element approached at sixteen degrees and squeezed the metal element, I encountered disasters. It proves the theory of five-element theory, which functioned amazingly when we used that to predict fortune.

Basing on that experience, I read two horoscopes that had the combinations I mentioned above and people related to that both died. I could get through the difficulty because I had another planet that carried earth balance with me at the time (earth exhausted fire and growth metal and canceled out the conflicts between the fire and earth).

Since then I continue to use this theory to predict fate for my friends. The results are amazing. I continue to use that principle to read charts. I learned a lot when I did it for my best friend Christin Ding.

Christin Ding and her husband, Andy, were both my master's friends who witnessed the amazing *Tie Ban Shen Suan* as well. They referred me to a lot of clients and forced me to read their horoscopes carefully. Christin Ding passed away in 2009 from cancer. I calculated her experience in the last two years of her life and got a lot of enlightenment.

In the beginning of 2007, she had an operation. I said she was okay then. However, according to the planets' movements in her horoscope, at the end of May to the twenty-sixth of June, she will have a bad experience. In the end of May, she started to have jaundice. A doctor made all the tests and did not know what was wrong. Before the twenty-sixth of June, they found out her bile duct had a tumor that made her bile spread over her body. Knowing the reason, a related treatment was used to release and released the jaundice.

Christin had a big operation in July, and things seemed good. But I told her something bad will happen at the end of 2007. She said I did mention an operation, and I forgot if I did. It really happened that doctor told her that they needed to do another operation and she must wait for a call. I figured that the eighteenth to twentieth of December she would have another bad experience. Until the seventeenth, the hospital did not call her, and they usually notify their patients a few days before the operation. She received a phone call on the eighteenth, registered on the nineteenth, and had a six-hour operation on the twentieth of December. Doctors did not do anything because the test results showed her cancer cells had already spread everywhere. However, after a few days, the hospital told her the test was wrong and having an operation still can help her. She spent another thirteen hours having the operation. That meant the six-hour operation on the twentieth of December made her suffer for nothing.

During those days, a few predictions based on the movement of the planets were proven right. In the bad day, I pointed out she had to wash her wound, and it bled a lot. She believed in me more than I believed in myself. Before she passed away, she still mentioned the accurate calculation I made to people around her. She is the one who knew me the best and helped me the most in my life. When I lost all my money in the future commodities investments, I hung out in her home. I had a good time there and felt nothing bad. I miss her and appreciate her very much. She hoped I continued the research.

However, since I already confirmed how planets influence people's life, I lost my curiosity to study it. I stopped promoting this book and let what will happen happen. We have no way to change the traits in the universe and stop the conflicts it creates—what do we worry for?

I remembered Shao's prediction about my father's children. It said that after being carved again and again, a *jade would be worth as much as a city*. My name Pikwah in Chinese means *light of a jade*. So far, up to today, I did not see any of my other sisters' achievements that matched Shao's comments. The experience I had was just like I was being carved. I hope my opinions in this book are valuable, and I hope that my success could prove Shao's greatness. His predictions were accurate up to my name *Jade*.

As a matter of a fact, Shao's prediction even involved names. It told the names of people who would benefit you and hurt you. I hardly saw my teacher pull out that kind of information. However, I once met a person who confirmed to me that in his life he worked for three different bosses, and they all had the same last name as Shao predicted. Things sound incredible here. However, many names were coded in the Bible and were recorded three thousand years ago. It is no wonder that predictions could be accurate up to names.

In ancient China, in order to determine the degrees of the planets, Chinese astrologers made observations on the mountain at night. Their predictions were based on that kind of research. According to the historical record, a famous astrologer, Chang Guo Lao (张果老), knew that he would have big trouble the next morning because a very bad planet was approaching the degree where his sign was. It really happened— the next day the emperor ordered him to drink some wine. It was believed to make people live forever, but it actually contained poison. After drinking the wine, Chang's teeth fell out and his nails turned black. Since Chang Guo Lao had expected something bad would happen, he and his assistant wore special clothes and set up special rituals that helped them counteract the occult force. They got through the crisis.

Chang also predicted that the niece of the queen would die right after being born because bad planets were in a bad degree for her. Their predictions also came true. Since those records relate to the palace, they were considered official records in China.

Those predictions related to planets involved with five element theory as well! I paid a huge tuition and confirmed that what our ancestor believed was right.

From January to February in 2020 A plague caused by Coronavirus spreading in Wuhan, China. I studied the conjunction of planets in 1918 when twenty-five million people were killed by the Spanish flu. I was surprised that in both year Jupiter was approaching jidu (the conjunction of the moon's orbit and the Sun's orbit). The Chinese consider that would cause disasters. Beside that they believed there is conflicts between Venus and Jupiter, as well as between Jupiter and Saturn. In 1918 July Jupiter was conjunction with Venus and in 1918. In the beginning of 2020 Jupiter was approaching Jidu and Saturn. The Earth had things happened as below: six earthquakes occurred in the world; two airplanes were cracked; Australia had big fire, Indonesia had a serious floods. African and South America had plagues. Spain and Canada had serious storm. Pakistan had avalanches. Philippines had a volcanic eruption. Plants in Africa and India was destroyed by 60 trillion famines. The U.S and Iran had military conflicts. Government of Russia resigned together.

It is interesting that in 2011, a Chinese Chen Guo Xian (陈国先) basing on the Chinese medical theory about lung, predicted that a there will be a plague from Dec, 26th 5:00, 2019 to March, 24, 10:00, 2020. An U.S psychic Silvia Brown mentioned man-made microorganisms in Wuhan in 2008 attack people's lung as well. Both predictions were published.

Data Relate to Spirits

For many years I collected data from friends and news sources that reported relevant topics. Most of these friends actually do not believe in the existence of spirits, even when they mentioned their supernatural experience to me. Their descriptions therefore are objective and trustworthy.

Spirits Tend to Show Up in Dreams

When we were sixteen years old, as Red Guards in China, we only recognized Marxist materialism. One day my classmate, Lin, told us that she saw an old woman dying in her dream. The next morning she wrote down the information to release her unpleasant experience. After one month, she received a letter saying that Lin's grandmother died the night when Lin had the dream. Lin had never seen her grandmother, a landlord who was exiled far from them. During the Cultural Revolution, even Lin's mother dared not contact her own mother. Lin's peculiar dream provoked our curiosity about the supernatural.

A friend, Wang, told me his experience when he was ten years old. During the Second World War, Wang and his mother rented a room near their family's barbershop to avoid traveling. Every night Wang would see a woman with long hair sitting in front of his bed. He could not help but announce that he saw a ghost and got hit by his mother because of that. The landlord stopped his mother and made no comments about what he said. Occasionally, he saw the landlord's family picture, and the women he met at night were there. The landlord finally admitted that her daughter was raped and killed by Japanese soldiers in the room that Wang and his mother were renting.

In 1978, my girl friend, Manyi, dreamed of her fiancé, who was in the US at the time. They had lost contact for years and became engaged when they heard from each other again. In her dream, her boyfriend was very upset, and they could not touch each other. One month later, Manyi received a letter informing her that her boyfriend died in a car accident that happened on the night she dreamed about him. A few months later she received a picture of her fiancé. He looked exactly the same as he appeared in her dream, with a bald head. The amazing part is that Manyi had not seen her boyfriend for over ten years, and she never knew that he was bald. That means Manyi had a realistic encounter with her boyfriend in the dream. If her boyfriend was only an illusion from her memory, he should not be a man with a bald head. Spirits are similar in appearance to their physical counterparts. What Manyi saw was her boyfriend's latest appearance, not what was an illusion in her mind ten years ago.

A friend, Weng, was an assistant movie director. He always laughed at my faith about the predestined and spirits. However, he changed his attitude completely after coming back from a trip. He could not wait to tell me his experiences. He and his team spent a few nights on an island to produce a movie. A few coworkers complained about being bothered by someone at night. Weng believed that they had illusions and influenced each other psychologically. One day he was chatting with policemen in their office, and they told him that a drug user died in the house where Weng and his coworkers were living. The police officer also confirmed that many people lived in that house complained about being bothered by that ghost.

A Hong Kong newspaper columnist once published his experience in Europe. He said they constantly heard strange noises in their hotel. One night he saw a woman who was guarded by a group of vicious people walk into his room. That women was beautiful but miserable. Her hands were cuffed, and she wore dresses with the style from the Middle Ages. They passed through the walls and disappeared from his room. The next day his friends mentioned a similar scenario, and he also saw those people cut off the woman's head. They found out that the hotel's address was used for executions during the Middle Ages.

Spirits might show up or manipulate some people, but stay away from others. My friend Yao told me his experience when he worked as a farmer. His two roommates always claimed to see a woman hanging in their room, yet Yao saw nothing. They later confirmed that a woman did hang herself in their room. Yao told me that even dogs were scared. They came close to him at night and barked for no reason. He never doubted what his roommates saw and believed that his aura was strong enough to reject ghosts. Yao is a tough-looking guy who had dark skin, big eyes, and a dominant demeanor.

Spirits Can Cause Accidents

My friend Dai's cousin Mu was incapable of getting to school on time regardless of the means of transportation he used. Random situations would set Mu back from reaching his destination. He looked like he was in a dream and was confused most of the time. A psychic declared that Mu was being controlled by the spirit of a dead child. The child had stepped on a glass bottle, and his neck was cut by one of the broken shards. The psychic said that the child was angry and tried to cause a similar fate on others. Mu was his next victim. After doing research, Mu's father found out that in their city two other children had died in the same pattern. Mu's father requested a ritual to free Mu from the spirit.

A friend's friend was killed by a car while in her seventh month of pregnancy. The driver ran a red light with an incredibly high speed when he made a turn. He was not drunk and had no reason to be in hurry. He just lost his mind at that moment. It was interesting that one year ago an infant right in that place was killed by a car accident.

In the spring of 2008, a train from San Tong China ran much faster than the speed limit. It went off the track and hit another train. The accident resulted in the deaths of more than eighty passengers and injuries to a few hundred people. It was the worst train accident in Chinese history. Nobody understood why the train traveled at that excessive speed at the moment. It is said, in January 2008, at about the same place, eighteen workers worked on the train track, and sixteen of them were hit and had died. The investigation said the workers started work too early, and there was a lack of communication with the oncoming train.

A friend of a friend, Zhu Zhu, was able to see spirits occasionally. When she was a teenager, she saw a male in her dreams frequently, and she always had a low fever which could not be cured by doctors. She did not take that seriously in the beginning, until one night she overheard a conversation that sounded related to her. One said, "She was mine, you cannot get involved." She realized that her dreams meant that she had been possessed by spirits. She got help from a monk who lit incense and prayed for her. She saw incense vibrate for no reason. Soon after that she saw the same man in the dream, and he told her that he had to leave her alone. Since then Zhu Zhu never saw the spirit again and recovered from the low fever. If Zhu Zhu did not get help from a monk but got help from doctors, she might need to take antibiotics or psychiatric medicine. Both of them could not heal her fever but created side effects.

When at her twenties, Zhu Zhu had another experience of being controlled by spirits after her mother returned from a trip. The spirits admitted that she met her mother on the trip and followed her back home. Zhu Zhu asked her mother if anything peculiar happened on her trip. Her mother revealed that the lights in her hotel room automatically flickered on and off one night and the Buddhists' recitations on tape turned off automatically.

Weird things began happening since then. Zhu Zhu wore a small jade Buddha, and the strings of her necklace snapped constantly for no reason. One day Zhu Zhu lost control all of a sudden. She didn't realize what she was doing, but she heard her daughter say, "Stop doing this! We are going to die if you don't stop." Zhu Zhu held her daughter and ran until she felt free and regained control of herself. She required help from the same monk and got rid of the spirit like before.

Years ago, a father from Queens, New York, killed his three children and claimed that a voice told him to do it. The voice said that if he wouldn't kill his children, they would die anyway. A son killed his father in a house where once the same incident happened. It seems spirits could control murderers and make tragedies happen again and again.

A mother from Brooklyn, New York, killed her son by smothering him and attempted committing suicide afterward. She was rescued as she tried to jump on to the subway tracks. She immediately told the authorities to save her son, but it was too late. She actually loved her son and had a happy marriage. That day when her husband called and asked how she would like to celebrate her birthday he heard the tragedy. The woman claimed that an unknown force controlled her and made her do that horrible killing. This is another case of possession rather than attempted murder.

A short time after my friend Mei got married, her husband began to act weird. One day he even tried to strangle her. At the moment of being strangled, Mei heard a woman laugh and say that her husband will be possessed and her marriage will be destroyed. Mei believed in what spirits might do and believed that her husband was unaware of his behavior at the time. Everybody convinced her to get a divorce. As her astrology consultant, I told her that according to their charts, her marriage had no problem, but their house had bad energy. Her husband either lost money in real estate investment or suffered from real estate investment. Instead of filing for divorce, Mei placed a lot of signs meant to ward off spirits in her home. Because of that her husband refused to go into their home, and that never happened before. He refused to go into churches as well. It looked like the spirit was controlling him.

Some years later I met Mei again. She told me that she was still married to her husband, who has recovered since they moved from that house. Her husband had a successful business that allowed her to stay home and take care of their daughter. She appreciated my support during those tough days. If we didn't believe in the existence of spirits, we would not be able to find a proper way to handle this kind of situation.

A newspaper once reported that two girls committed suicide on a railroad track. Those girls were optimistic and showed no tendencies of suicide. The day before they died, their schoolmates saw them talking to each other in high spirits. It looked like they were waiting for dates. When no one could explain the girls' motivation for killing themselves, I got an answer in the last paragraph of the news. It said that *the girls laid on the track where two boys were killed by a train some time ago.* I believe that the spirits of the two boys confused the girls and made them believe that they will be able to date those boys by committing suicide.

Someone once fell down and died in the subway station near my home. I was worried that the spirit of the deceased would cause trouble. It really happened that within three years, four people died on those tracks. One of them was a student who played on the subway platform and fell onto the tracks.

A newspaper reader reported his experience in the Second World War. Once he saw a little girl sitting in front of a big house and crying. He was impressed because it was dusk in a cold winter, and the girl only wore a red short-sleeved shirt with white dots. He felt sorry for the little girl and believed that she was a servant who was mistreated by her master the owner of the house. The next morning, he heard that someone in that house jumped into the river.

The victim was a blind and deaf old lady who kept saying that someone was calling her that night. Family members of this old lady ignored what she said because they heard nothing. They all believed that the old lady jumped into the river when she lost her mind. The news contributor found out later that two years ago a little girl drowned in the river near that big house. When she died, she wore a red short-sleeved shirt with white dots, the same outfit that he saw. He thus believed that the girl's spirit did show up that night, confused the old lady, and made her jump into the river.

Once I studied a coworker's horoscope and asked if she had some bad experiences in 1983. She said "Yes!" and told me the following story.

That year, she had already finished her master's degree, and her boyfriend was taking his PhD courses in Hawaii. Her boyfriend constantly heard a voice telling him to jump out of windows. One night he really jumped off a cliff that was about ten feet high. Surprisingly, he did not get hurt, except for his eyeglasses, which broke. Without eyeglasses, her boyfriend was able to drive home safely on a road that he was not familiar with. The spiritual voice he heard seemed to mislead him as well as protect him. He had to register himself in a mental hospital to avoid jumping out of a window again.

It is lucky that the PhD student believed in the existence of spirits. He told his girlfriend to get help from a monk who was on a trip in Hawaii then. During that bad year, my coworker had to share her boyfriend's pressure dealing with an unknown entity. She had faith in which no one believed to save her boyfriend. She was running around in Hawaii, an unfamiliar place to her, looking for a monk whom she never saw, and helped him get into a mental hospital where monks were not allowed to practice. The monk put his hand on her boyfriend's head. The young man felt a cool energy escape from his body. The next day her boyfriend was released from the mental hospital. His doctor said, "You are fine now. I do not know what made you recover, I only know that it was not our medicine."

Her boyfriend finished his PhD degree and taught in a college in Hong Kong. If they had not gotten help from the monk, he would have been treated like a mental patient with a severe mental illness, and his nervous system would be retarded by psychiatric medicine. It is the concept about spirits helping him stay away from a permanent disaster.

Spirits can confuse our minds and cause tragedies to happen. In January 1999, a mental patient, Andrew Goldstein, pushed a passenger onto the tracks of the New York City subway. He claimed that a cool energy entered into his body, and all of a sudden he had an irresistible impulse to push the passenger standing next to him. Apparently, he was controlled by something at that moment. However, the jurors did not believe in the existence of spirits. They assumed that Andrew Goldstein was supposed to know the difference between a wrong and right action. They convicted him of murder. A mental patient, Andrew Goldstein, will be jailed for almost the rest of his life.

A famous British biologist, Lyall Watson, did plenty of research on supernatural events. In his book *Beyond Supernature*, he reported the healing results of psychics he witnessed. A weird illness made a young Filipino boy have two different physical appearances. His right side was a nice young boy's body. However, his left side was covered by scars and wrinkles and looked like an old man without energy. Teeth in the left side of his mouth were bleeding and stuck out; meanwhile his left eye kept excreting wax. Suffering from pain, he could only walk slowly. He never left the Philippines all his life, yet he could speak one kind of African language.

For three days a psychic used different ways to heal the little boy, such as yelling at the boy loudly and throwing something into the fire. In the rituals the little boy screamed and whipped himself. When the boy collapsed on the floor, some green flames burned in the fire. The next day the boy no longer spoke an African language, and one week later his skin, teeth, and hair were all recovered. It was said the boy's face appeared weird three years ago in a car accident, and his mother was killed during that.

Mr. Lyall Watson also mentioned another girl's face became unbelievably ugly all of a sudden, and no medical treatment could heal her. She got help from religious ceremonies. In front of a priest the girl talked in a strange voice saying, "This child is mine!" The priest had to fight hard against something to make the girl recover from being retarded and ugly. It is interesting that the girl had those symptoms after seeing her mother lose her mind and kill her drunken father with a knife. I believe that spirits not only possessed those two children in the above cases, they also are the major medium that caused those fatal accidents to happen and killed their parents. Spirits are much more powerful than we could imagine.

As a scientist, Dr. Lyall Watson's report should be very trustworthy. Spirits can cause accidents by confusing people's minds. Actually, in many cases, people do claim that they were told to commit murder or suicide. That is why psychiatrists always ask their patients if they hear a voice or see something weird. Unfortunately, they simply believe that mental patients have illusions but never believe that their patients were being harassed by spirits.

There are many incidents of people claiming to have dealt with the supernatural beings through Ouija boards. Many claim to have been possessed by the spirits that they communicated with during their Ouija session. In the game, players slightly lean their hands on something such as a plate. The plate will move on the board indicating answers that the players ask. Those questions usually are about the future that is usually only known by spirits. Some players were sent to mental hospitals because they were insane through their interactions with the spirit world, yet despite that, authorities still don't bother to alleviate the problem through restrictions and limitations. It's amazing how the board is still sold as a toy after these incidents. We desperately need to reevaluate our theory about psychiatry. They should recognize the concept of spirits to enforce and enrich their treatments.

Spirits Can Convey Messages

Spirits usually communicate with humans through dreams. The data they give us in dreams sometimes is amazingly correct. My friend Jaska's mother once dreamed of Jaska's departed sister. In the dream her daughter said that she hoped to marry someone from somewhere. Jaska's mother visited the address that she obtained in the dream. It was interesting that at that address, a man with that name died years ago.

The last time I saw Su she was smoking in her bed, and that was right before she committed suicide on a train track. For a few months she had smoked days and nights, and nobody knew that she was planning to commit suicide. A few days after she died, three members of her family dreamed about her. She told them that she was fine in the other world, and death was not horrible at all. In my opinion, those dreams were related to the spirit of Su rather than the dreamer's illusion. It was impossible that different people had the same dream in the same night. No one can control people's subconscious to create dreams like that.

My friend Chan dreamed about his deceased father, who complained that his environment was too wet. Chan visited his father's grave and saw that it was flooded.

Cases below were published in newspapers in Taiwan. A woman was missing in a river, and for three days her body could not be found. She showed up in her sister's dream complaining that she was cold. According to her indication, her sisters dropped her clothes into the river and followed them. The clothes stopped floating in front of a big rock, where the victim's dead nude body was buried.

Another man disappeared in a flood. One night his wife dreamed about him and was told that he was a few hundred miles away from their hometown. His wife contacted the policemen even though it sounded impossible. The man's body traveled a few hundred miles along a river. He was buried without being identified until his wife had the communication with him in the dream.

A man from Taiwan had the same dream after having an accident on a lake. In the dream a woman admitted that she did try to make him drown in the lake. She changed her mind at the last moment because she needed him to contact the police department. She claimed that she was murdered in the same lake a while ago, and her case was considered an accident. The man could not stand being bothered by the same dream constantly like that and contacted the policemen. Surprisingly, they did have a case related to a woman drowned in a lake. A man went rowing in a boat with his girlfriend and later reported that the girl disappeared. The girl's body was found in the lake, and the whole case was considered an accident. The man's weird dream made the policemen reopened the case. The victim's boyfriend failed to explain why he did not ask for help immediately when his girlfriend was drowning. He finally admitted that he committed the murder.

It is interesting the accident that the man encountered was at about the same location and same in the afternoon when the woman was killed. The man survived miraculously and had a dream that revealed a real murder case. There is an important meaning here: if the spirit of that female victim had not changed her mind and made the man die, we would consider that was merely an accident. *People refuse to attribute the cause of the accidents to spirits even though accidents occur with the same pattern and in the same place again and again.*

A report from the *New York Chinese World Journal* (November 19, 2007) gave us a lot of enlightenment about how spirits make accident happened. In five days, between November 13 to 18, 2007, the same train, number 1034, caused accidents three times in a row. The first accident happened on November 13. The second one happened on November 16, and the third one happened on November 18. All three victims were crushed like meatballs and couldn't be identified. All those accidents happened in the same place, Taizong City, as well as at about the same time, 7:00 p.m. The train was about to leave Taizong City for the north.

In Taiwan, since 1968, three airplane accidents occurred on the same day in three different years—February 16. The first accident was on February 16, 1968, and it caused eighteen passengers to die. The second one on February 16, 1986, and all thirteen passengers on the airplane died. The third one was on February 16, 1998, and caused all 196 passengers to die. The years 1986 and 1998 were both the Tiger year in the Chinese calendar. All the accidents happened in the same pattern at the time when the airplanes were landing.

A half year before the accident of 1968, the airline company printed a calendar that listed its service schedule for the whole year. Having been reviewed again and again before being printed, the schedule of March and April 1968 still were omitted due to negligence. Under no circumstances would things happen like that. It was interesting that the airline did suspend service in March and April 1968 after the accidents happened on February 16. It looked like some entities had already known the accident would happen and they made things happen again and again. The powers of spirits are much stronger than we realized. To prevent tragedy from happening, we may have to know how to communicate with them and to comfort them.

Another news item also related to a murder case. A man kept dreaming of a woman who complained about being murdered. The man asked policemen if there was such a case. Police officers confirmed that a female mental patient did jump out of a window a while ago and that it was considered a suicide case. Since a man who knew nothing about the case had a weird dream, police reopened the case. The police investigated people who lived near the suicide scenario. A witness claimed that at the time the woman "jumped out" of a window, he saw someone standing behind her. The victim's boyfriend was scared because the message was conveyed from a stranger's dream. He finally admitted that he was a murderer who pushed the girl out of the window. He worried that if he did not confess, he would receive more punishment from the spirit of his girlfriend.

A detective told us his experiences. If victims were clenching their fists when they died, their murderers would be found eventually. I believe that people who died unwillingly usually had stronger willpower than people who died from natural causes did. Their willpower can influence a detective's thinking, giving them inspiration to find the murderers.

In December 2003, my coworker Mrs. H slipped on the subway platform. One of her legs was squashed into the gap between the train and the platform. Her entire leg was blue and purple for two months. Mrs. H was the psychic lady I introduced previously in this book. I asked her if she had any dreams about this serious accident. She said no. However, she told me that she was constantly bothered by the same terrible dream: *In the streets, a lot of buildings collapsed, and dead bodies were everywhere.* I thought it must be another attack by the terrorists. I even mentioned Mrs. H's dream to my friends. Mrs. H had the same kind of eyes that David Copperfield had. From them I could tell that she had psychic ability since birth. She thus could easily feel Mr. Benny Hinn's energy transmitted through the TV. She admitted that she had healing power and psychic ability that other people did not have. When her friends were sick and she touched them, they felt better. What she wished always came true, such as her enemy would have bad luck eventually. She told me for that reason, she tried not to hate her enemies, but to pray for them and hope they would change their behavior. She did not think her psychic ability was inherited and attributed it to God. Either way, God's gift made her a faithful Catholic, and that faith returned to reinforce her power.

Once, Mrs. H asked me if I knew a certain kind of Chinese green tea. She knew its name from an angel in her dream. She told me that kind of green tea could heal the illness in her respiratory system. I never heard that tea she mentioned. Since there are so many type of green teas in China, I did not think I could find what she wanted. A few months later, she walked into an Indian store accidentally. She saw some tea packed in the same box and had the same name as she saw in the dream. The tea did improve her health amazingly.

Another thing that happened to Mrs. H was also unbelievable. When she immigrated to the United States, she was a poor single mother with three children. One day she was very sick, could not work, and had no money for food. When she prayed to God for help, a fifty-dollar bill floated into her apartment through the window and dropped right in front of her. I do believe what she said because I once heard a similar demonstration performed in Hong Kong.

Spirits Might Determine a Person's Whole Life

I knew Ming through a tenant who was an antique consultant for Ming. My tenant was a greedy antique dealer and never gave good advice to anybody, but he helped Ming collect antiques everywhere. It looked like he was driven by something.

The antiques he collected bought in good money for him all these years when he worked as a cook. I didn't know his birth time and could not tell his fortune from his astrology chart. In my opinion he should not be that rich unless something special happened to him.

I told Ming my opinion one day. I asked if he lost some loved one in his life and got financial compensation because of that. Ming was a quiet person who kept his privacy well. Hearing my comment, he could not help but tell me his story. It was started from the prediction of Mr. Chan, a famous blind psychic in Hong Kong—the one who once visited my teacher and whom Shao said can communicate with spirits.

Many years ago, Chan told Ming that he would have a son in his late thirties and that son would die young. That loss would also end his first marriage. Ming then said, "It is all my cousin's fault." I was confused by his accusation. A fortune-teller's prediction coming true means that we cannot avoid what happens in our life. His bad luck should have nothing to do with others. How could he blame his cousin? I did not interrupt him, and I let him continue his story.

In his childhood, Ming had a cousin. The last day they saw each other, they had a big fight. His cousin changed the plan they made earlier, ignoring the two movie tickets that Ming had bought, and went to the beach alone. When Ming got home from the cinema, his father beat him without any explanation. Later Ming found out that his cousin drowned, and people thought he was also on the beach.

A few years later, Ming's aunt dreamed his cousin said that he hoped to marry a girl. He wanted Ming to bring a chicken to congratulate him on their marriage. Ming refused to follow the instructions, but his aunt did. She followed the address she obtained in the dream and found out that there was such a girl, but she was already dead.

In his thirties, Ming really had a son who was very intelligent. As a five-year-old boy, he could understand lectures from third grade. Unfortunately, he had an abnormal heart. One night Ming dreamed his cousin, who accused Ming of taking their son and said that they needed him back. To compensate Ming, they would help Ming make money.

Ming was scared and woke up from the dream. He suggested sending their son to the hospital, but his wife refused to do it. At that moment nothing seemed wrong with their son at all, and there was a big snow storm.

The next morning, when Ming got to his office, his boss told him that his son had already died in a hospital. Ming told me his son straightened his legs and died within a few minutes. He believed it was his wife's fault because she refused to send their son to the hospital. When they stayed together, they could not help but miss their son. That tragedy ended his first marriage.

For the last twenty years, Ming invested in eight different restaurants, and most of them made a good profit for him. He was the one who looked for the restaurants' locations and signed the rental leases. There were two locations he did not like, but his partner insisted on renting them, and those restaurants end up lost money.

At the time I talked to Ming, he was retired but traded in the stock market. He never researched any company's background because he didn't know English. It was amazing that once in a while a name of a company came to his mind, and that stocks of that company would help him to make good money.

In Ming's life, many things looked like coincidences, but they were predestined or were arranged by some power. Sooner or later, scientists would be forced to recognize the existence of spirits. It will make people behave themselves more. A Chinese quotation reminds us that "God or spirits are watching us from three feet away." Spirits really exist, and they are more powerful than humans. They not only see what we do but also know how we think and make us pay for our sin.

Part Three

After This Book Was Published Online

Physicists and Psychics
Respond to This Book

After publishing this book online, I sent out about two thousand emails and a thousand postcards to different universities. Most of them were sent to the math or physics professors. I thought they were familiar with Einstein or Hawking's theory, and they will be interested in what I said. So far altogether only one response was received and less than twenty books were sold.

I sent a book to Stephen Hawking and told him that I was knocking on the door one by one to find information that people do not know. If he understood my meaning and gave me a hand to promote my opinion, it will save my time and energy. Since I kept mentioning my hopes, his secretary threatened to block my email. A while later, he sent me an email saying that Dr. Hawking will read my book within a couple of days. It made no difference to me anymore. I did not expect that he will give me a response. Many years after that, I noticed that he mentioned our universe could be created from nothing when he mentioned his M-theory.

He started to believe that things can be developed through different formats, not just one format as our scientists allowed. He also believed it is difficult to make predictions about things. He at least gave a break to astrologists who hope to predict things and their predictions are off the facts sometimes. I jump up to comment on the Big Bang because I felt that for proof of the infinity situation, that Einstein's formula implied to create the Big Bang story, is ridiculous. I do not belong to their field and was not intent to follow the other things they said.

My mother recalled that when I was three years old, I took a fifty-yard trip alone, asked a twelve-year-old girl to play with me and accept me as her friend. That girl said no! I cursed her on every step I walked home and fell on asleep because of exhaust. Fifty years later today I did the same thing. I finished only two basic physics courses, yet I hung out in the physics fields and told people how I thought. I cursed when they rejected me. It looks like they started to adjust some of their theories about the Big Bang today twenty after I published my book.

For contacting those people, I registered in an astronomy club and received a lot of emails from its members right away. They exchanged information excitedly, telling about the location and the movement of the planets. It looked like they enjoyed their research very much. I knew nothing about what they said but sent them emails one by one. I reminded them to figure out how the movements of planets impact human's life. If they did that they will have the most important achievement in the scientific fields. They can gather big attention from the public instead of just getting entertainment in a small group. Those people stopped sending me emails immediately.

I also wrote letters to Professor Richard Gott, astrophysics professor from Princeton University. His article "Chess and the Laws of Physics Excerpt for Time Travel in Einstein's Universe" in Physics Central Writers Gallery got my attention. He believed that "in time travel researching space and time warped in unfamiliar ways" could create something "we have never seen," "a pawn reaches the other end of the board and it is promoted to become a queen." "Our car could tunnel out of a closed garage and suddenly sit out on the lawn." He confirmed that phenomenon has been shown to be true on the subatomic scale.

His conclusion is agrees with the so call paranormal events amazing. I wrote four letters to remind him about that consistence and got no answer from him. Maybe he did not want to contact people who are superstitious.

I did receive one response from a professor at Virginia State University. I sent him a book, and in return he wrote me a short review. He has been teaching quantum mechanics for over ten years. He told me that he could not see the relationship between my theory and quantum mechanics. However, my book gave him an enlightenment for the glimpse he had in the supernatural fields. He said science is a beautiful tool to interpret things, but something in this world obviously is beyond being explained. He told me he read my book carefully and some chapters he read more than one time. He even referred my book to his coworkers and his students.

I made further discussion with him, told him that life events seem to have uncertain consequences, and that made me think of the uncertainty principle. I also told him that I never actually study quantum mechanics. I thought it related to something that is too thin or too diluted to be attracted by gravity. Phenomena could show the supernatural when gravity was absent at the moment. I hoped he did not simply cut the connections between the physics theory and supernatural. Scientists should explain supernatural events instead.

Again I received no answer from him. I was disappointed and deleted his email address. I could not recall his name, was not sure of the school he worked for, and didn't save what he wrote to me. From 2003 to 2004, my two thousand emails and one thousand postcards created three thousand disappointments for me. A professor from a state university once recommended my book to his students and coworkers. That was the only merciful feedback from the scientific world—a field that I am concerned with.

In 2005, David Cheung, a professor of the physics doctoral faculty of the City University of New York, provided some verification of my theory. He believes that my book is about the philosophy of science and can be a guide for the future. He referred physics documents to me that seemed to agree with what I believed. I list them below to back up my opinion.

1. Li and Gott from Princeton University believed that in certain cases, particles might be surrounded by a negative mass shell so the total mass of the particles will be zero (Li and Gott, physical review letters, Vol. 80, 2980, 1998).

2. Barrett: There is good reason to suppose that our best physical theories are false (Philosophy of Science 2003, pp. 12061218).

As a physicist professor, Dr. Cheung finally gave me supports in some ways but still not do it openly. In 2003, with great hope I handed him my book. When he returned it, he typed a short paragraph in a big white paper without putting his name down. He said my book only met statistical requirements but not scientific requirements. He told me that he didn't mind that I showed his comment to somebody because that paper had no signature on it. The way he handled things made me feel that our scientists dare not comment on theory that this world doesn't recognize. No wonder I received no response from them. I threw Cheung's comment in the garbage can before I finished reading it.

In 2005, I met Dr. Cheung again, and he admitted that my book was the only book that was placed on his desk and he had read it *several times*.

I repeat my points to him again: Physics recognized that water can exist in three kinds of states. As solid, ice, it can hardly move itself. It exists as an object that does not allow our fingers to get through it. The second state, water, exists as liquid that can flow and has lower density which allows our fingers to put in it and feel it. The third state is gas, which moves faster than water and our fingers cannot tell their existence. How about things are beyond the state of gas and move even faster could not be caught by the graviton. Because their density is lower than gas, they could not be detected by particle detectors. Their zero mass lets them become nothing, and that is what the Chinese mean, yin.

After that discussion, I was able to get more information from Dr. Cheung. I asked him which Western scientist displaced a yin-yang symbol openly. He emailed me the yin-yang pattern that was carefully designed by Niels Bohr. Bohr showed it on his coat of arms when he was awarded by the Danish government. Scientists were surprised and confused by his actions. He never explained why he respected a Chinese philosophy that much.

Dr. Cheung tried to find out if any formula related to yin-yang theory gave enlightenment to Bohr's theory. I told him that we didn't need formulas here. The transformation between the yin and yang is exactly what quantum theory tries to explain. Isn't that enough to make Bohr admire this Chinese philosophy?

Dr. Cheung told me that Werner Karl Heisenberg, the scientist who found the uncertainty principle, was Bohr's student. Gott and Heisenberg both are from the Planck Institute in Germany. I am glad to hear that the scientists who attracted my attention all belong to the same group. I know almost nothing about science, and my instincts helped me choose the scientists I like. It is amazing that they are all from one group.

Dr. Cheung also told me that Gottfried Wilhelm von Leibniz, the founder of the binary theory of computers, once received a book written by a Chinese man named Shao. A Western priest surrendered it after returning from a trip in China. The name of Shao is very rare in China, and there was no great scientist in Chinese history with that name. Dr. Joseph Needham, a famous scholar in England, had a book that introduces Chinese science and civilization (SCC). He mentioned that Shao Kang Jie's theory had a crucial influence on the founders of modern science.

Dr. Cheung referred me one quantum paradox: a particle pair might carry information at a speed faster than light. It shows that when one particle is being measured, the other particle knows it instantly regardless of their long distance separation. He said that this phenomenon was discovered many years ago. Scientists hardly research it because it challenges the traditional laws of physics.

Dr. Cheung is the only physicist who discussed physics problems with me, and he is also my former brother-in-law. I don't know if I should consider this help from the scientific world or from someone I know, my ex brother-in-law.

All my life I believed that people working in the scientific field had the most freedom. They are enthusiastic and cannot wait to seek the truth because that is what they live for. Maybe I was wrong. Scientists are just like people in the business world. They care about their jobs and paychecks more than anything else. They thus rather defend the traditional theory that agree with the majority's opinion. They tend to avoid disputes and making no comments on rules that were not being recognized by the scientist world.

Psychics' Predictions
about My Book

O n New Year's Eve 2006, my friend Lee called me. The first sentence
  she said was "You will have a lot of money. Don't be *afraid to keep
whatever comes. You could make some donations if you think the money
is too much for you.*" I was surprised about what she said because I
never asked that kind of question, even deep in my mind. Those words
sounded like it came from her lips, not her thought. She then told me
that she knew I was depressed, and that was why she made the call.
She herself felt odd by what she said as well. She then made a further
explanation: "*When good luck comes you can't stop it. The whole world
might listen to you then. I don't want you to miss the chance and hope you
will go as far as you can.*"

Lee was a smart, strict, and moody lady whom I knew for over
twenty years. She expressed her meaning accurately, never exaggerating
and was amazingly correct. She simply told you what she thinks
without extra words and never repeated herself. She didn't care about
how you feel. She usually commented on you, criticized you, or gave
you a warning but hardly said things to please you. Her phone call
made me feel that she had a special sense about something or she was
by an entity to comfort me. I have three reasons to believe so:

In the New Year's Eve, I was extremely anxious and frustrated when
Lee called me. I was looking for a partner and waiting for his phone
calls or emails minute by minute, and that seemed would never come.
Writing the book exhausted all my energy already, and I then realized

that the difficulty had just started. I have to confront embarrassment. The more work I did, the more despondent I got. That night I was lying on the sofa alone, thinking about if I should accept the ending of my life and not expect that much. I started to believe no matter how many good things might happen in the future, it could not offset the misery that I had by carrying this obligation. The suffering was so great and will last forever. Lee's speech made me feel that some entity sent her to comfort and encourage me.

1. Lee told me to donate some money that was kind of related to my worry. I never disclosed to her that, for a few times I felt I received a message saying that I might lose my love or health if the book is selling well.

Even though I worked ten years on my book, I still refused to use my health and happiness to exchange for the book as a bestseller. What do I need the money for if that money could not bring love and health to me? I wrote this book just because I have no choice—I am the witness who knew Shao Kang Jie's greatness, and I had to tell this world a great truth. I spent so many years figuring out the predestination of life. The conclusion I finally had was so important for all of us. Theoretically I should not give up my goal even though my life will be shortened. I was worried and hated this kind of situation: losing my happiness and shortening my life in exchange.

2. Lee never read my book, but she said, "The whole world will listen to you," which surprised me. Lee did not even finish high school. However, she can always get to the right place at the right time and grab the chance. Her psychic ability and her knowledge about feng shui helped her accumulate ten million dollars in assets. She only cared about business, not complicated academic concepts. Therefore I never mentioned Einstein's formula and the Big Bang theory to her. She didn't know any of my opinions in the book but said that *the whole world will listen to you*. She made a comment later explaining

why my book can bring in profit because there are other markets in this world, not just the market of the United States. Both comments are amazing for me because I believe the scientific, political, and economic points in my book are strong enough to attract attention worldwide. Again, Lee never read my book or knew my points. She never tried to please other people by saying untrue things; she just states what she believes.

Lee took astrology courses from me many years ago. At that time I was also practicing chi gong. Once in a while, I received some messages that I had no way to confirm. Worrying that I might go crazy, I stopped practicing chi gong. One day, without my requesting it, Lee commented about things that exactly agreed with the messages I received. She made me believe that my feelings regarding something were not from my illusions. Since then I noticed her psychic ability but never asked her about that.

Her prediction about my book caused my curiosity and asked if she actually predicted things correctly in her life. She told me her experiences as below.

Once, her husband asked her to tell the fortune of a friend who came from a well-known family in Hong Kong. With that kind of background he got everything he needed in his life. Lee refused to make any comment in front of that person. She told her husband afterward that his friend would die soon. A few weeks later, that young man killed himself by jumping out of a window.

She visited a house that was on sale. There was a hole in the front yard, and water came out from there. According to Lee's feng shui knowledge and psychic feelings Lee predicted that the master of that house would die soon. A few months later the master of that house really jumped out of the window and killed himself. He was facing an investigation because of corruption.

Lee once predicted that a cancer patient would not live to November. That man died on October 31. Once a guy made her pay but did not finish what he should do. Usually she did not allow things happened like that. She told me that she let the guy go because she felt that something really bad will happen to him. A few days later that guy died for health reasons.

Besides Lee, a psychic Jenny from California also made predictions about my book. She was referred by my client Mandy. Mandy called me once in a while from Reno. She liked to visit psychics and believed that Jenny was the best one she met.

For example, Mandy requested a reading for her sister. Before she mentioned the purpose of her visit, Jenny told her that her sister was buying a house and that house was very bright. One week later her sister informed her that she had already bought a house, and she liked that because it had a lot of sunshine.

Another time Mandy wanted to know how she would get along with her supervisor who was going to take a six-week maternity leave. Jenny said that her supervisor's maternity leave would be about five months, and after that she will quit her job and never come back. Later, things really happened like Jenny predicted.

Mandy's experience made me curious. I sent my picture and requested a reading from Jenny. The first thing Jenny talked about was my book. She told me to promote it on college campuses because she saw professors, scholars, and students were reading it. She said the book was on the college reading list. She could tell the book did not sell well when I self-published it online. She saw someone publish it the second time, and she saw more books were being printed. She saw I went from between colleges to give speeches. Down the road she saw a man putting a cap on my head in a ceremony. The ceremony looked like the same as her son's graduating ceremony when he finished law school. It looked like they gave me an honorary doctor's degree. She said she saw I was writing a second book and someone was helping me to do that. The second book sold faster than the first book.

It is interesting that she said when someone starts to help you, more and more people will be involved. That was exactly what I expected. I am not only selling a book, I am launching a movement. I did send her a book and told her to not read it before giving me the reading. She made the appointment for the next day. I didn't send her part four of the content that I am going to add to the book, yet her prediction made sense. I believe more people will come up to help me because of the nonrevenge movement I promoted and the new society I pictured in this book.

She also told me that she saw my great-grandmother from my mother's side helping me all these years. She was a quiet woman who felt proud to see what I had achieved. My strength and wisdom were from her.

Up to today I cannot confirm anything that Jenny said. I just record everything here in black and white and see what will happen. In my mind Lee and Jenny are very great psychics. If nothing comes out true, that means my faith about psychics and destiny is wrong. I will put my faith away, shut my mouth, cover my book and go home. Even though nothing Jenny said can be proven correct up to now, I still want to record why I think her comments are amazing:

1. Jenny had no time to read my book before she made the reading. Even if she did, I don't think she could catch my points so quickly. I always believed that scientists should like my book more because there is something new and important for them. Reminding scientists to research astrology is the reason I wrote this book. That is why 90 percent of my email and postcards were sent to universities when I promoted it.

By reading the book title *Why Life Events Are Predestined and How Our Universe Originated*, no one would believe that this book will be accepted by the academic world because scientists refused to discuss paranormal events in the last few centuries. Without reading my book Jenny said that people in college are starting to accept my opinion. Her prediction agreed with my expectation, and that is why it surprised me.

2. She mentioned my great-grandmother, which also surprised me. I just met my grandmother for a few short times in my life

and never have my great-grandmother in my mind. However I do feel that I was pushed and helped by someone when I wrote this book.

I have no any scientific background. All my life I only took two basic physics courses and never read magazines that published in English. One day I had nothing to do in a courthouse. I killed time by reading a magazine that I found next to a garbage can. From there I picked up the message of the zero point field version and phenomena of tunneling. Because of that I started to put them in the astrology book I was writing. After reading just one article in a scientist magazine, I joined the scientific discussion and brought my astrology researching to a scientific level.

I never read philosophy books after I was twenty-five years old. To write this book, I spent half a day reading the history of the philosophy that was written in Chinese. Among five hundred pages that listed more than one hundred philosophers, I noticed Descartes—the same day I picked up his book *The Meditations*, an English edition, in the library. Within five minutes I found what Descartes said, "*Spirits are subtle air or wind, connect our organs, and are seated in the pineal gland of our brain.*" I only made a copy of that paragraph and never read his whole book. Based on my English level, I don't believe I could pick up a philosophy and a reference of what I needed so quickly. Something must've made me do it.

The first and only time I read current scientific information online, I saw Gott's assumption accidentally, and I knew right away that his opinion was in the same track as my book. Even though I received no answer from him, I knew my opinion should make sense even to the scientists. I always believed discussing scientific problems is not my business. We have people who get paid to do it. I didn't keep the magazine I found in the courthouse. When I self-published my book, I even put *tunneling as turning*. I didn't know how to verify it and could not have any advice from anybody. It was amazing that my book did have some thoughts on physics. One day I walked into the library without a schedule or a plan. I stood in front of the bookshelves. Among hundreds of books, I picked up a thin book with only eighty pages. That book briefly explained Einstein's theory to young readers. Within five minutes, I caught what *Einstein believed. He said, "A stone was a stone only when it got in the gravity field."* I could not realize the greatness of such a saying until one hour after I left the library. Einstein left us a room to assume the stone might not show as a stone we saw before it dropped into the gravity field. So, what would it look like when it was out of our scale, such as the subatomic scale?

Stephen Hawking once said that we have had little success in predicting human behavior from mathematical equations. That comment has the similar wisdom as Einstein. They both leave room for our research. They never assumed that they knew everything and things they not know do not exist or are not true.

I actually had already given up writing my book in 2001. After my mother passed away, I reevaluated my mother's life. She had achieved nothing except raising her children. If I do not do anything, as my mother's daughter, I not only wasted my own life, I would waste her life as well. I picked up the writing again not for myself, but for her. I never expected that besides my mother, there was my great-grandmother's expectation as well. Jenny told me my great-grandmother was helping me all the time. I inherited her smile and wisdom. I think Jenny might be right because I did look like my mother, and she might look like her grandmother. My motivation and my English are not strong enough to make me finish a book that covers different kinds of topics. I do believe that I was guided by someone when wrote it. I did research later and found out that my great-grandmother's last name was Lee. She came from a wealthy family that had only my grandmother as her daughter. She received a very good education at her age. She died in her fifties when the Japanese invaded China. She could not fulfill anything and might have good expectation toward her descendants. The burden I carried is so heavy.

3. Jenny said that I was creating karma for myself. Just from that comment I believe she had psychic ability. I never heard the word *karma* and almost ignored it until my friend Mandy explained it to me. Karma means deeds a person did in his past life that might affect his next life. The book I sent to Jenny was an old edition, which did not discuss world affairs at all. The discussion about science or the paranormal had nothing to do with karma. Only when I suggested how to negotiate with our enemy and how to solve the messes in our economic and health-care field did it involve karma. It is amazing that Jenny knew my ultimate goal without reading the last part of my book. She even said that more and more people will help it . . .

Reason to Republish This Book
Again and Again

The last time I promoted this book was in 2011 when college students occupied Wall Street Square in New York City. I went down there a few days a week after finishing work. I hung out in the square looking for media people to introduce my idea of managing our society. I stood in front of the video which connected the internet and promoted my opinion. During those days, things I was concerned the most was not related to the predestination of life events but about how to stop the wars and solve America's financial problems. I recommended retirement homes and promoted a new standard to measure success—the ability to use the minimum material to obtain the maximum joys. Today, in 2025 it is still the priority subject I concern.

I stopped promoting this book since 2011 because I was exhausted, I encouraged myself used broken English to introduce my retirement plans. After hanging out in Wall Street Square I went home alone in the cold weather and then sent my proposals to senators and congressmen one by one in front of the computers. I got no response at all and all of a sudden I felt that I actually was talking to the wall. Seldom books were sold and the psychic's predictions did not come true. I decided to keep my promise: covered my book and went home. I thought it's the world's lost if people don't know life are predestined.

I even do not know since when my book was not unavailable in the market anymore because the publishing house went out of business. Ten years after, someone told me my book was research in the highest rank in Amazon, over ten thousand readers once looking for it. She convinced me to republish it.

Just as the psychic Jenny's predicted, in 2020 I plan to publish another book, " *An Appeal to the U.S Supreme Court and A Proposal to Our President*" . The book is about an estate court case related to my son's grandfather, Sydney Fields. He altered his will after his third wife died. He was ninety-six years old and in an audiotape recorded by Vanguard, he claimed that he could not read typed words in documents even with a magnifying glass. His statement was supported by a doctor's note as well. However, the will drafter Edward Curtin insisted that Sydney could read. He admitted that he never read the will aloud in front of witnesses. Still his will execution was considered duly by Judge Mella. That "will" distribute all his nine million dollars to five relatives of his third wife and left the Fields family nothing. That will also cut Sydney's donation charities from four million dollars to 1,500 dollars without the testator's explanation.

The will drafter also sworn that " beneficiaries got those inheritance because they were considered as family members by the testers. Such an important sworn was accepted by the judger and was actually dismissed in the court hearing. They used a forged initial to substitute the page with the all the will provision. They also presented a note to supported their distribution ratio. That note, mentioned nothing about altering a will, only listed numbers and names. The most of all it does not look it like was written by a ninety-six-year-old blind man. Over all the will provision had no tape record back up but only had the will drafter's confirmation and the related sworn was dismissed by the will drafter afterward. Still the judger basing on that to make her decision.

Our appeals was denied seven times by four courts within three years. Felt disgusting for the experience in a democracy country I decided to publish it brief to a book with the title of " An Appeal to the U.S Supreme Court and A Proposal to Our President" and republished the book of " Why Life Events are Predestined and How Universe Originated"

In both books I presented my proposal about how to reducing government's debt by building retirement homes or communities. I concerned stopping wars more back then.

I remember in 2001, America started two wars for what happened in 9.11. In the name of capturing Osama Bin Laden, Bush bombed both Afghanistan and Iraq. To avoid being bombed, the Taliban power once agreed to send Bin Laden to the UN but not to the United States. Bush's Government refused the suggestion. In January 2006, Bin Laden again suggested negotiations. The Bush Administration again rejected this immediately with the reason of America will never compromise with terrorists. It looks like some people in and behind the U.S government meant to maintain wars and make bloody money.

In May, 2011, Osama bin Laden was killed in Abbottabad, Pakistan, during a raid by U.S. Navy SEALs. It prove that America didn't need two wars to make the revenge. The United States spent over $8 trillion on the post-9/11 wars, and these conflicts have resulted in an estimated 4.5 million deaths. Out of that 7000 were America soldiers and the wars cost big protests by the American.

In 2021, warmongers are more clever. Instead of sending American to die they support Ukraine to resist Russian. Their politicians openly declared: most American government's funding to the war actually was left in the United Stated, paid to U. S Military - Industry Complex. No American solder was died when Russia is being exhausted. Now they make Ukraine use their land and minerals to pay money was spent in the war, 300 billion$ and Ukraine said that they actually received only 80 billion dollars.

Another way for greedy money drug manufacturers. American is the only country in the world that makes biochemical testing. The Covict-19 virus helps American's vaccine in good sell, Government paid over 100$ to each shot when all the American were forced to take it. Those greedy people behind the Deep State always have some ways to spend taxes payers' fund with beautiful reasons. Work together with politicians in the government they don't have any monitors.

In 2025, guiding by Elon Musk , doge find out huge corruption and waist in the Federal government. They believe they can save one trillion government budgets. Under the pressures only ten percent of that expenses was deducted.

Reason to have the "destiny" concept

I am not only concerned about the predestination of life events and the origination of our universe. I also care about the practical meanings of such a destiny theory. An academic discussions will have no any meaning if it cannot influence our religious, economic and political world. Our society is filling with messes created by the selfishness of religions and the greedy of warmongers. Humanity needs new concepts to guide our behaviors and needs new interpretations for the meaning of a successful life.

We need scientists to confirm the existence of gods and spirits, entities related to quantum from the other dimensions. They are more powerful and watching everything we did and how we thought. We therefore have to behave ourselves. We do not need to act extremely nice to the others. All we need to do is to treat the others with the way that we want to be treated. You love your homeland, so don't destroy the other people's homes. You don't like to be bombed, so just don't bomb other people. You don't like other people to have nuclear weapons, so destroy the nuclear weapons that you have. You like money, so give other people a chance to make money. You value your life, so please don't send other people to die. Otherwise you will not be blessed by God no matter how much you wish to be.

Basing on the Chinese astrology theory, what we deserve in our lives are predestined. It determines by the balance of *our birth time traits* that are composed by Yin, energies seeking in the universe then.

It just likes an equation has a fixed sum that add up by our wealth, happiness, and health. Over taking wealth could result that person's happiness and healthy will being reduced. Warmongers who become rich through the endorsement of war must eventually suffer or cause their children suffering for the fortunes they over took.

Entities from the other world can turn curses into reality by invoking life-threatening events, like choking on a cracker or causing someone to become an alcoholic. They can even make someone die of a heart attack. If they skipped the punishment their descendants will take that for them, sick or never happy in their lives.

What need to be Changed?

In 2008 when I republish this book Obama used " change " as his campaign slogan. I thus add discussions about what needs to be changed in my book. Below is my opinions then.

Political Changes

We should have only one political goal, should be to stop all the wars, anti-poverty and build up a harmonious world on the earth. To meet our goal, we should reform terrorists instead of eliminating them. Pulling troops out of Iraq and putting them in Afghanistan is not a real change. The real change is to negotiate with our enemy without conditions. We should deem all wars to be illegal, including wars for democracy and wars for eliminating nuclear weapons. We should switch our goal from securing our homeland to maintain peace in the world. Our homeland will not safe only until hateful are eliminated in the world. If you launch a war to secure your homeland, it means someone else's homeland will be destroyed.

I once watched a news channel showing how a group of Middle Eastern people waved flags and walked to a man who was about to shoot with a gun. Those people, fearless, shouted loudly and seriously to the gunman. In front of their determination the gunman finally put down his gun, like a scenario in a movie. Those brave Middle Eastern men risked their lives to obtain peace in our real lives and in front of cameras. They proved to the world that peace can be obtained through negotiation. I am sorry that I forgot the date of the newscast. I always remember those people and believe that they are the people who deserve the Nobel Peace Prize. We should give them the highest honor for things they tried to do and eventually accomplished.

To end the conflicts, we should learn how to forgive. We should encourage terrorists to put down their guns and help them survive by doing business trades. We can give them a piece of land to settle them down. We can also encourage the new generations to communicate on school campuses. When our youths love each other, warmongers and selfish religious leaders cannot make us fight.

Economic and Ethical Changes

When I was in college, I told my economics professor that seeking a higher GDP and encouraging consumption actually lead our society to throw things away. He gave me a C for the comment I made. However, what happens today proofs that I was correct.

All these years, encouraging consumption has been the basic principle that rules our economy. We believe that spending money can create jobs and prosperity. For that reason, our government, private businesses, and individuals spend more money than we have. This is how the financial crisis happened.

Unfortunately, in the age of free trade, stimulating consumption could not bring the unemployment rate down. Attracted by the low cost of labor, our manufacturers move overseas. Losing jobs and having great debt, Americans blame the Chinese for control-ling the currency rate.

Actually, the Chinese are also victims of the financial crisis. In China, 60 percent of GDP was contributed by foreign investors.33 Many products that are labeled "made in China" actually are merchandise of American companies. In the production process, Chinese only obtain1 to 3 percent net profits as the laborer providers. That means their blood-and-sweat earnings were canceled out when the US dollar was devalued by 6 percent. In reality, US dollars have already gone down 20 percent versus RMB. The two trillion US treasury bonds and US dollars the Chinese are holding created a huge loss for them. China has no choice but to use a government-controlled currency rate, and they were widely criticized by America.

Our consuming behavior has been wasted hugely on earth's resources. It could not create jobs like we expected but created a huge debt for our government. It is obvious that resources on the earth cannot make 7.5 trillion people have unlimited consumption

Actually, the capitalist invisible hand running by consumption and production cannot provide jobs that our a few billion on earth population needs. We should take into consideration a happiness index rather than high GDP. We have to change our standard of measuring success and prosperity as well. A successful life should lie in spending the least raw material resources and be able to experience the highest pleasure.

To change people's concept of seeking for profit, our media should endorse unselfish people rather than wealthy people. In the Iraq War, an American soldier covered an exploding bomb to save four of his fellow soldiers. In the Virginia Tech shooting, a professor held the classroom door closed in order to let his students escape through the window. A fourteen-year-old student in the Bronx High School of Science in New York sacrificed his own life and pushed his classmates back to the seashore. Over ten thousand Australian construction workers volunteered to build housing for people who lost their homes in the fires. They practiced the principle of yang (cede) and even gave up their lives for others. They provided a sharp contrast to those ugly warmongers and greedy CEOs from Wall Street.

In order to set a new moral standard for this world, we need to make the whole society have contempt for greed. Instead of reporting news about movie stars, our media should disclose the names of those greedy CEOs and warmongers. When they die, they can't take their fortunes with them and left sins for their descendants.

Combine Capitalist and Socialist Systems

We have to reevaluate our so-called capitalist system. All these years we believe that the capitalist system is better than the socialist system because it gives freedom to individuals. People in the capitalist world can criticize their government without being jailed. They can share business profits through stock investments. Our government collects taxes to take care of the needs for the public and the society. However, if we make further observations, we can see that taxpayers cannot prevent warmongers stealing the taxes payers' funds by selling weapons in wars. We cannot stop CEOs from taking "bonuses" from the stock market. We have to pay whatever the oil companies and health insurance companies charging us. Our tax fund is applied to support poor people without the government's careful control. Our social security funds are drying up, and the retirement age is postponed again and again. The public's benefit is being corrupted when our politicians making big talks.

The US Government plays the role of collecting taxes and spending money only. The businesses they own such as the post office created only a huge deficit. It is because starting at the same wage rate the government's employees receive 30 percent to 50 percent greater compensation than the private employees and maintain poor efficiency meanwhile. The poor people are taken care of well in this country. However, all the funding they spent are from taxpayers or from the government's debt, not from the government's investment. We have been relying on the government's debt to offset conflicts between the poor and the rich in our country. However, we cannot live on debt forever like that. The capitalist system is facing the end with the debt problem of all the Western countries.

To solve the problem, we have to add the socialist model to our capitalist systems. Our government should not give tax cuts to those oil and insurance companies who deal with the public. Instead we should set a profit limit on those fields which already have great privilege. The net profit they make cannot exceed the rate that our regular businesses make—that is around 5 percent. Every dollar over the limit has to be surrendered to our country as taxes, or they could choose to step down and let other people get into the field.

We have to add capitalist concepts to the government's projects as well. The government should not just carry nonprofit policies. Instead of giving out bail-out money, we have to invest the funds to create a profit first and use that profit to help the society in the long term. In the next chapter, I will further discuss this subject.

How to Solve Employment Problems

The most noticeable stimulus strategy Obama's team created was Cash for Clunkers. In the summer of 2009, the US government gave out $3,500 to $4,000 vouchers to each consumer who replaced his or her vehicle. The strategy cost taxpayers a total of 3.5 to 4.5 billion dollars and benefit the car manufacturers from both the domestic and foreign countries. The policy made car sales increased 15 percent in the beginning and declined with the same percentage one month later. Four billion dollars was given away with no profit return. The policy cost huge money but only helped 1,350 union employees return to work at General Motors and about the same number of positions were created in other car companies. In this way Obama created a ten-trillion-dollar debt in his presidency which is not less than little Bush spent on war.

Obama has ignored new problems in the age of free trade and simply complained about jobs were moved to overseas. He didn't realize that businessmen only care about profit, not job creation. Facing high salaries, health insurance, and rent costs in the United States, manufacturers prefer to go somewhere else for better deals. Unless we improve our investment environment, they won't come back.

Improving the investment environment means reducing salaries. Hourly salary rates that American motor companies pay to union workers are about twenty dollars higher than what the Japanese motor companies pay to their American workers and thirty to forty times higher than rates in Asia. It results in American motor companies losing money on every single car they sell.

Along with bringing down salaries, we have to bring down rent, health insurance, and college tuition. Reducing salaries must be along with reduced consumption. All these years the Americans made high consumption and had low production. We created the largest trade deficit when dealing with the other countries. It is time to pay back for the luxury time we have had and reduce our consumption.

Basically, we have two ways to solve the unemployment problem. The first way is what we are doing now, stimulate consumption and support GDP to increase jobs. So far in 2009, the government spent 1.4 trillion dollars and obtained no obvious result. Another way is to cut working hours. If mankind could maintain a happy life with low costs, we do not need to work for that many hours. When jobs are shared, requirements for that will be decreased in the market and will leave jobs open without creating government debts.

1. Let people share all the government jobs. In this way the unemployment rate will decrease at least 5 percent. In 2008, the average salary and benefits that New York City employees had were one hundred thousand dollars annually. Such amount can be shared by a few employees and support two to three families. Under a bad economic situation, the taxpayers' fund should be used to support as many people as possible. We would not decrease people's pay rate, just reduce their working hours. The luxury times they gain can be used to enrich their lives and compensate their financial loss.

2. Build up retirement homes and encourage early retirement. We have a hundred million Americans over fifty-five years old, an age range that the Chinese retire at. If 2 percent of them were willing to retire earlier, it would have left two million jobs open. Obama's team once spent 4.5 billion dollars on Cash for Clunkers and only created a few thousand temporary jobs for motor vehicle companies. With the same amount of money,

we can build a thousand retirement homes which have one hundred units of each. That can allow a hundred thousand people to retire and leave their jobs open permanently. The construction process will create another a hundred thousand jobs immediately.

To save our economy our government should not simply give money away. We should invest the same funds and make a profit first. The easiest way is to build up retirement homes in one time and collect rent in long term to offset set set certain social security payments. In this way government can become a big landlord instead of just releasing pensions. According to an estimate, rent for a unit in a retirement home is seven hundred dollars. In thirty years one hundred units in a retirement center will make twenty-five million dollar incomes for our government and the construction cost is only five million dollars. (using Musk's box house may cost even less) People who received social security checks can be government's potential tenants. All we need to do is building houses in the suburbs, and set up facilities that have low-cost entertainment programs. Let people enjoy life and home care of each other over there .People who have their own houses but hope to move in to the retirement home could sell or rent their own apartments in the city for pocket money. Those who have no properties can work part time to earn their pocket money.

It is stupid and shameful that we postpone the retirement age to seventy when our society needs jobs. Our youths carry huge student loans and find no jobs, while our senior citizens have to work with sickness till die. My coworker has very high blood pressure, weighed over 250 pounds, and feels pain all her body. She can hardly move but still has to do home visits at her job. Her father died young. When she thinks she could not retire until she is seventy years old and that she might die before that, she tears up.

Actually, people who retire at fifty-five years old can provide home care to the people who need it in the retirement home for exchanging for the same service when they get old. In that way we saves huge home care expenses for the government. Today, the government creates home care jobs for people and provides the same services to the same people when they get old. Average it proves few thousand dollars for each person monthly.

Managing retirement homes is a real challenge. The government can provide different levels of retirement homes to people based on their social security incomes. They can dance, cook, play poker, have computers classes, plant organic vegetables, chess, chat online, etc. Buses from the retirement homes can take them downtown and arrange trips once a week for them. People can register with friends to move in there. They can also transfer to different retirement homes in different states such as Hawaii, Florida, and New York. They can enjoy different environments and not just as a prison, living in one place until they die.

I once read a senior citizen's article in a newspaper disclosing that living in a senior citizen home was just like living in heaven for her. It was even better than living with her children. Another article described a beautiful picture when foods from different countries were prepared at a senior citizen's center on a holiday. When people are getting old, having company is more important than having money. It is said some American universities did build retirement homes for their alumni. People there live eight years longer than the average people The medical expenses they spent were 30 percent less. This is why building retirement homes is a practical idea.

To minimize the management cost, we can set up connections between retirement homes and colleges. In that way funding that the government spent for the retirement homes can be used as students' financial aids. It gives students chances to practice what they learn in school such as business management, social work, and even medical knowledge. The energy of the young people will lighten up the retirement homes.

To avoid insurance costs, people living in retirement homes have to give up their right to sue the government. We set up all these things basing on trust and loving. People who refuse to retire would not receive any social security payment until they are seventy years old.

Sharing jobs and encouraging retirement might result in reducing people's income and consumption. Again, it will give people more time to enjoy lives and compensate for their financial loss. *Our final goal is to let people live well.* As long as our people have shelter, food, company, and enriched lives, our goal is met.

In today's day, we can have low-cost entertainments easily such as having contests for sports ,chess, poker or having a party in the park. We can also find soul mates and chat with new people through the internet. That kind of activity needs time more than requiring money. We do not need to seek for high consumption and high GDP as long as we can have food from green resources . *If we can still live happily with a lower income, then sharing jobs and retire earlier will be a practical idea. The job requirement decline in the market will help us solve the unemployment problem.*

3. Build up facilities near factories and farms where prove jobs for lower salary for people who enjoy facilities for free in some way, such as Musk's box houses and AI doctors, free bus transportation. Low salary rate will encourage more manufacturers move back from overseas and provide jobs. People who need public assistance must work and live in there. Government's welfare system and manufacturers are co-operation in this picture and give people what they need. Government can even share profits with the manufacturers and maintain the expenses they need in the facility.

Set up facilities is more efficiency than repairing roads, bridges create no direct profit but spend money. When those projects are finished, there will be no more jobs unless the government prefers to maintain those jobs forever. On the whole, the government should not act as a nonprofit party. We should run government projects with capitalist concepts, invest it, and make a profit. We should promote concept of thrift and learn how to live well with low income. A successful life should be able to obtain the most happiness and spend the least resources on the Earth.

Seeking for consuming materials in 2010, US national debt is almost 12.9 trillion dollars, and in 2019, our debt was over twenty trillion dollars. In the summer of 2025 the debts reach thirty six trillion dollars. It will increase one trillion dollars every 100 days. It is the consumption concepts and unfair distribution system create the problems. Capitalists create jobs in overseas for lower salary pay. The poor refuse work and live in welfare system. Things are not happening as capitalist designed a few hundred years ago. Things need to be changed as soon as possible.

Actually, humanity's surviving should not rely on consumptions and jobs created by invisible hand on the market. We should depend on land, green resources which creat food forever. Land can provide all we need rice, vegetables, fruit, cotton and feed animals we need. Humanity have been lived on the earth from generation to generation without being backed up by industry and financial institutions. We will have our basic needs if we keep our land as rich organic soil. We don't need to emigrate to the Mars but should stand firmly on the Earth, a gift that God created for us. This is the only planet that allows us to enjoy lives.

How to Decrease Medical Costs

In 2010, Congress gave the final approval to Obama's medical reform bill. It is said the bill will help thirty-two million people get insurance and reduce $ 100 billion government's deficit in next ten years. However, it doesn't have details about how to work things out. The bill cares about where to get fund to cover the insurance rather then how to control the medical cost. In over two thousand pages, the bill hardly mentioned the word *doctors*.

American's total medical costs in 2009 were $2.5 trillion, 17.3 percent of its GDP. Each person spent $8,047, three times of the cost in developing countries. In 2018, enrage cost increased to $10,000 and the performance of U.S. health-care system was ranked thirty-seventh in the world. Meanwhile American's life expectancy was ranked forty-second. The premiums for an individual's health insurance can go up to $1,100 per month and still 62 percent of personal bankruptcies contributed to medical debt.

The government's Medicare costs have doubled up every four years. In 2009, U.S. Medicaid cost was $250 billion dollars, 25 percent over the budget and thirty-seven times more than when Medicaid was started.

I don't think Obama's medical reform is successful only when it actually reduces medical expenses in this country. Below is my proposal in 2011 about how to work things out. Some of them might no longer important because we will have AI doctors soon. I keep my opinion here as a record and proof that many things can be done on decreasing government's medical cost and we didn't do it.

1. It is said by proportion America's doctors and nurses are much less than most of developed countries. We actually can release more medical licenses, shorten the medical education period and reduce its tuition. The government can financially aid medical students make them provide services later as return.

2. Government should set up quotes and ceiling price to monitor medical expense instead of paying whatever bills they received. Medical expenses have limited by quotas. Such quotas can be rolled over to the follow year or transfer to family members. should directly control health-care premiums and use them for treatment purposes only. We should laminate the compensation for medical lawsuits. The government can monitor medical services by suspend doctors' licenses. People who refuse to give up suing rights must pay higher premiums.

3. Reduce the management fee in the medical field. Today 31% of our healthcare fees are used for administration that is double the overhead in Canada. We can also pay a low salary to unemployed people and lay off those who do not do their jobs.

4. Promote the theory of preventive medicine. People who accept substitute treatments, such as herbs and acupuncture, can pay lower premiums. People saving high quotes can pay low premiums as well. We should allow terminally ill patients to end their live peacefully instead forcing them suffer and pay high medical bills.

We have many ways to cut down the health-care costs. Nothing was done because some parties are making huge money from our medical health system. If we do not stop what them in time our government and our social security system collapse.

Time to Untie Science
and Religions

In our academy fields, all these years scientists avoid to encounter religious scholars even though many successful scientists believe in God eventually. It is time to apply scientific theory such as quantum mechanics to proof the existence of God. Our faith is basing on scientist concept not basing on the doctrines religion leaders promoted.

In history, wars that are caused by religious conflicts were much more prevalent than any other wars. When Muhammad promoted the Koran, he believed that only the God Allah deserved to be venerated but not any other divine beings. For that reason, he launched wars to kill people. Killings related to this kind of arguments continued for a few thousand years. The fighting even existed between the disciples of Mohammed, Sunnis, and Shiites.

The same dominant attitude is in the Bible where has many pages encouraging killings. For example, in the Old Testament (2 Kings 10:15), Jehu killed seventy sons of Ahab and killed all the worshippers of Baal in Israel. The Lord said to Jehu, "Because you have done well in doing what is right in my sight and have done to the house of Ahab all in my heart, your sons shall sit on the throne of Israel to the fourth generation."

In the Old Testament (Sam. 14:51), the Lord also told Saul to attack the Amalek. "Kill both man and woman, infant and nursing child, ox and sheep, camel and donkey." Saul only killed all the humans but did not kill all the animals. For that reason, Saul was rejected by the Lord. Solomon married foreign women, and he was accused by the Lord as well. The first few commandment of Ten Commandments tell people that they can only venerate one God. and this causes killings between people who have different faiths. That make its other Commandments such as not to kill, not to rape, not to steal, and not to occupy the other's house will turn out to be empty talks. **It encourages a lot of religious wars meanwhile, such as the Jewish being killed in the second world wars and they kill the Arabs in Gaza as return today.**

to them. They let people think and act in stupid ways such as become body bombs. In the name of the Law of One, RA material had comments about a priest. Mankind should think and rethink about those meanings and reconsider the difference between the Law of One and the Lord of One. Today religious people create wars to force people to believe in their only Lord.

If scientists can prove that the Creator, gods, ET, and spirits are real in the scientific world, all those religious leaders will lose their rights of instructing people. Mankind has to behave itself because entities in the four, five, and six dimensions are watching

God created humanity and provide a beautiful earth to support our life. We not appreciate things we have but using God's name to create religious wars. If we set up our faith basing on scientist quantum mechanics we will respect all entities from the other world. We will behavior ourselves for we are they are watching us. It is said entities from the other world can communicate each other as one. Their principle is " Law of one" and we misunderstand it as " Lord of one". For such Lord of one " disciples of Yahweh, Catholic, Jesus, Christianity, Mohammed, Sunnis and Shiites fight for a few thousand years and kill each other without mercy. All they want is to make people respect their own God.

Thing happened in China are different. With the concept of Yin Yang theory, the Chinese believe all God and spirits are real existence. They respect them and never fight for religions.

The Chinese culture, Chinese medicine theory, astrology theory, Fengshui, Chi Kong theory and Dao's magic are involved with Quantum mechanics. I spent ten years to write this book is for rehabilitating the reputation for the Chinese science. China not just have four inventions, compass, gunpowder, paper and typography, we have much higher theory that humanity still don't know. This culture should be promoted by our government. It is sorry that scholars don't get help officially but being accused of superstitious and put into the jails.

This book, *Why Life Events are Predestined and How Our Universe Originated* was first published in 2001, twenty-four years ago. This is the fifth time I published it and I submitting homework that I finish in my life long. I am glad that some of its concepts have been recognized by scientists. The experiment named by "Manhattan" is kind of admitted by government. However, we still have long way to go, such as how to explained the Universe, how to protect the Earth and how to eliminate humanity's greedy and manage this society. I am at my seventies now and all jobs must be fulfilled by your guys. We don't need be rich in materials. We just need to live in a smart way, with healthy happy and peaceful but without natural disasters. Let us pray for that.

June 10th 2025 in New York City Flushing

References

1. Hawking, Stephen. "Annihilation between Particles and Antiparticles," *A Brief History of Time*.
2. Hawking, Stephen. "An Astronaut Fell into a Black Hole," *A Brief History of Time*.
3. Cowan, Thomas Dale. "Daniel D. Home," *The Book of Séance*.
4. Descartes. "We have our souls seated in the pineal gland of our brain," *Meditations*.
5. Time Life Books. *Mysteries of the Unknown, Psychic Powers* (1987) p. 92.
6. "Empty space is seething with energy," *Discover Magazine* 19 (August 1998): 78.
7. Hawking, Stephen. "Grand Unified Theory," *A Brief History of Time*.
8. Weiss, Brian L. *Many Lives, Many Masters: The True Story of a Prominent Psychiatrist, His Young Patient, and the Past* (1988).
9. Hawking, Stephen. "Hawking's Radiation," *A Brief History of Time*.
10. Valentine, Jim. "Healer Removed Tumors," Psychic Operation (American correspondent).
11. Wheeler, John A. *Psychic Power*, 60–61.
12. Moody, Raymond A. Jr. Life review, p. 6, *The Light Beyond*, p.11, lines 7–11.
13. 13 Henry, John. "Isaac Newton willing (cont.)," *The Scientific Revolution and the Origins of Modern Science*.
14. Cowan, Thomas Dale. "Physical Objects Shown in a Séance," *The Book of Séance*.
15. Deavy, Terry. "Philadelphia Experiment," *The Philadelphia Experiment*.
16. 16 . A Chinese book written by an important Chinese officer who once was in charge of all the recent chi gong research in China Sheng Jiang, "Pills Pass through Sealed Bottle," *The Confusions*.

17. Process of moving things by willpower, *The Confusions Caused by Heaven*.
18. "Pyramids," Discovery Channel.
19. Hawking, Stephen. "Questions about the Big Bang That the Physicists couldn't answer (cont.)," *A Brief History of Time*.
20. Rhines, Joseph. *Psychic Power*, 60–61.
21. Chi gong master saw ancient honorific arch in meditation, Chinese book introduces chi gong, written by chi gong master Li Hong Chai.
22. Hawking, Stephen. *Structure of Atoms*, books written by Hawking.
23. Hawking, Stephen. "Steady State Theory (cont.)," *A Brief History of Time*.
24. "Tunneling," *Discover Magazine*, 76, 140.
25. "Yoga Experts Still Survived after Being buried for a Few Days in India," *Psychic Operation*, chapter 5.
26. Psychic Power, *Voyage of the Titan* was written in an interesting way, 79, 11.
27. Messing, Wolf. "The Physic," *Psychic Power*.
28. "Zeropoint Field Version of Physics," *Discover Magazine*.
29. Burrows, Gideon. *The Arms Trade*, 152.
30. Geller, Uri. *My Story*, 279.
31. Geller, Uri. *My Story*, 268.
32. Buckland, Buckland. *The Spirit Book*, 119.
33. *Chinese Economy in Ten Years*, CCTV financial news department.
34. *Chinese Economy in Ten Years*, CCTV financial news department.
35. Elkins, Don, Carla Rueckert, and Jim Mccarty, *Law of One*, 207
36. Elkins, Don, Carla Rueckert, and Jim Mccarty, *Law of One*, 201
37. Elkins, Don, Carla Rueckert, and Jim Mccarty, *Law of One*, 196
38. Coburn. Senate.gov

www.ingramcontent.com/pod-product-compliance
Lightning Source LLC
Chambersburg PA
CBHW021629120626
46545CB00002B/467